How to Communicate Evaluation Findings

Lynn Lyons Morris
Carol Taylor Fitz-Gibbon
Marie E. Freeman

Center for the Study of Evaluation
University of California, Los Angeles

SAGE PUBLICATIONS Newbury Park/Beverly Hills/London/New Delhi

Copyright © 1987 by The Regents of the University of California

The second edition of the *Program Evaluation Kit* was developed at the Center for the Study of Evaluation, Graduate School of Education, University of California, Los Angeles.

The development of this second edition of the CSE *Program Evaluation Kit* was supported in part by a grant from the National Institute of Education, currently known as the Office of Educational Research and Improvement. However, the opinions expressed herein do not necessarily reflect the position or policy of that agency and no official endorsement should be inferred.

The second edition of the *Program Evaluation Kit* is published and distributed by Sage Publications, Inc., Newbury Park, California, under an exclusive agreement with The Regents of the University of California.

For information address:

SAGE Publications, Inc.
2111 West Hillcrest Drive
Newbury Park, California 91320

SAGE Publications Inc.
275 South Beverly Drive
Beverly Hills
California 90212

SAGE Publications Ltd.
28 Banner Street
London EC1Y 8QE
England

SAGE PUBLICATIONS India Pvt. Ltd.
M-32 Market
Greater Kailash I
New Delhi 110 048 India

Printed in the United States of America

Library of Congress Cataloging-in-Publication Data

Morris, Lynn Lyons.
    How to communicate evaluation findings / Lynn Lyons Morris, Carol Taylor Fitz-Gibbon, Marie E. Freeman.
        p. cm. -- (CSE program evaluation kit, 2nd ed. ; 9)
    "Developed at the Center for the Study of Evaluation, Graduate School of Education, University of California, Los Angeles"--Verso t.p.
        Bibliography: p.
        Includes index.
        ISBN 0-8039-3134-4
    1. Evaluation research (Social action programs)   2. Communication in the social sciencess.   I. Fitz-Gibbon, Carol Taylor.
II. Freeman, Marie E.   III. University of California, Los Angeles. Center for the Study of Evaluation.   IV. Title.   V. Series: Program evaluation kit (2nd ed.) ; 9.
H62.M648   1987
361.6'1'072--dc19   87-21752
                         CIP

SECOND PRINTING, 1988

Contents

Acknowledgments

The preparation of this second edition of the Center for the Study of Evaluation *Program Evaluation Kit* has been a challenging task, made possible only through the combined efforts of a number of individuals.

First and foremost, Drs. Lynn Lyons Morris and Carol Taylor Fitz-Gibbon, the authors and editor of the original Kit. Together, they authored all eight of the original volumes, an enormous undertaking that required incredible knowledge, dedication, persistence, and painstaking effort. Lynn also worked relentlessly as editor of the entire set. Having struggled through only a revision, I stand in great awe of Lynn's and Carol's enormous accomplishment. This second edition retains much of their work and obviously would not have been possible without them.

Thanks also are due to Gene V Glass, Ernie House, Michael Q. Patton, Carol Weiss, and Robert Boruch, who reviewed our plans and offered specific assistance in targeting needed revisions. The work would not have proceeded without Marvin C. Alkin, who planted the seeds for the second edition and collaborated very closely during the initial planning phases.

I would like to acknowledge especially the contribution and help of Michael Q. Patton. True to form, Michael was an excellent, utilization-focused formative evaluator for the final draft manuscript, carefully responding to our work and offering innumerable specific suggestions for its improvement. We have incorporated into the *Handbook* his framework for differentiating among kinds of evaluation studies (formative, summative, implementation, outcomes).

Many staff members at the Center for the Study of Evaluation contributed to the production of the Kit. The entire effort was supervised by Aeri Lee, able office manager at the Center. Katherine Fry, word processing expert, was able to accomplish incredible graphic feats for the *Handbook* and tirelessly labored on manuscript production and data transfer. Ruth Paysen, who was a major contributor to the production of the original Kit, also was a painstaking and dedicated proofreader for the second edition. Margie Franco, Tori Gouveia, and Katherine Lu also participated in the production effort.

Marie Freeman and Pamela Aschbacher, also from the Center, contributed their ideas, editorial skills, and endless examples. Carli

Rogers, of UCLA Contracts and Grants, was both caring and careful in her negotiations for us.

At Sage Publications, thanks to Sara McCune for her encouragement and to Mitch Allen for his nudging and patience.

And at the Center for the Study of Evaluation, the project surely would not have been possible without Eva L. Baker, Director. Eva is a continuing source of encouragement, ideas, support, fun, and friendship.

—Joan L. Herman
Center for the Study of Evaluation
University of California, Los Angeles

Introduction

The purpose of this book is to help you communicate the evaluation information you have collected. The book contains prescriptions and advice to help an evaluator provide information that will be *usable* and *used* at many stages of a program's development. The suggestions and comments offered in this book are based on the experience of evaluators at the Center for the Study of Evaluation, University of California, Los Angeles and on advice from experts in conducting and reporting evaluation in many fields of social science and education.

How to Communicate Evaluation Findings has four chapters. The first chapter sets the context for communicating evaluation results. The main concern here is who needs to know what, and when? The chapter explains the evaluator's reporting responsibilities with respect to different audiences and uses to which the information may be put in formative and summative evaluations. The chapter includes general principles for maximizing an evaluation's impact.

Chapter 2 reviews various forms for communicating findings. It is a compendium of pointers for specific media such as memos, technical reports, news releases, informal conversations, and public meetings. The purpose of Chapter 2 is to help you present the results of your work in the form and style which will most effectively convey the message of your evaluation to primary and secondary users.

Chapter 3 helps you take advantage of the old adage "a picture is worth a thousand words." It describes how to develop tables and graphs. Relying heavily on examples, it contains prototypes of graphs and tables for displaying evaluation data. To assist you with oral presentations, the chapter describes a step-by-step procedure for preparing audiences to read and interpret graphs.

Chapter 4 presents a fairly standard and probably familiar technical report outline. Depending on the stringency of your reporting requirements, you may or may not decide to follow this rather formal method of presenting your evaluation and its results. You can follow this outline to the letter, or you can simply use it to become familiar with the set of topics that should be discussed in an evaluation report. The outline is intended to be exhaustive of the type of information that can be conveyed to an evaluation audience. A glance at Chapter 4 will show you that each entry in the report outline is accompanied by a set of questions. These questions are intended to clarify each outline section and to help stimulate you to write. By answering the questions in sequence, you will produce an outline of an evaluation report.

You have great leeway in deciding what to report and how to communicate the information. Evaluation is an evolving field, and there are few universally accepted procedures for collecting or for reporting evaluation findings. There is serious doubt, for instance, about whether most audiences can tolerate the deductively logical but usually dry presentations dictated by the classical report outline in Chapter 4. You are challenged to come up with effective presentations of your own. Your task as evaluator, after all, is to provide the best possible information to program funders, staff, and others you have identified as having a personal or professional interest in the program's processes and outcomes. Your obligation, therefore, is to gather the most highly credible information possible within the constraints of your situation and to present your conclusions in a form that makes them most understandable and useful to those interested in the evaluation.

Keep in mind, however, that the prescriptions and advice offered in this book represent communicating and reporting strategies possible *under the most advantageous circumstances.* Few evaluation situations, of course, match the ideal, and you will need to adapt this information to your own situation and political realities. Reading this book should at least help you to organize your thoughts about what you want to communicate and how you will deliver your message.

Chapter 1
Who Needs to Know What, and When?

You do not want the results of your evaluation efforts to go unused. All that hard work should not end up buried in a filing cabinet while the deficiencies of an ailing program continue, or the strengths of an effective program go unsung. Evaluations are conducted for a variety of reasons, but ultimately the main purpose is to provide information for decision making. Although many have bemoaned evaluation's impact in this area, fortunately there are concrete steps you can take to increase the chances that your findings will have some influence on the complex puzzle of program development and policymaking.

In the first place, you must consider the full process of decision making and the most influential actors in the program you are evaluating. You also should to be aware of the various potential points in their decision making process at which information is likely to be helpful. A single final report usually will not suffice to satisfy all purposes nor can you delay concern for reporting and communication until your data are all collected and analyzed. Rather, attention to effective reporting and communication must be ongoing throughout the entire evaluation process, from the initial planning stages to completion of your final commitments. The effectiveness dimension means also that you may have to report different kinds of information to different individuals or groups in different forms at different stages in the evaluation. Who wants to know what and when they need the information are key planning concerns, but facilitating the usefulness of your work requires even more. This volume expands upon three fundamental rules of reporting which will increase the likelihood that your evaluation findings will be used and not ignored:

- The information must be communicated to the appropriate potential users.

- Reports must address issues which the users perceive to be important.
- Reports must be delivered in time to be useful and in a form that is clearly understood by the intended users.

This chapter provides some practical suggestions for identifying and communicating with your primary evaluation user(s) and your most important audiences. Some of the tips may sound rather "political." They are. *There is no such thing as an evaluation free from political considerations.* Some of the suggestions about effective communication are fairly standard advice; no doubt you have heard them before. But familiar as they may be, the reminders are nonetheless very important.

Before focusing on potential evaluation audiences and messages, however, it is important for you to have the responsibilities and expectations of your own role as an evaluator clearly in mind.

Evaluator's Role

The nature of the evaluator's role with respect to the program will determine the content and format of your communication plans. The *Program Evaluation Kit,* of which this book is one component, is intended for use primarily by people who have been assigned to the role of *program* evaluator. This means that your primary responsibility is to collect and communicate information about the effectiveness of a program, as opposed to collecting information about the quality of a specific individual's performance. To whom do you communicate this information, what do you communicate, and when and how? Identifying these specifics will be an important concern from your very first contact with evaluation sponsors. Volume 2 in the Kit, *How to Focus an Evaluation* by Brian M. Stecher and W. Alan Davis, suggests how to handle these vitally important initial planning activities. Through exchanges with the sponsors and other key audiences or users, an evaluator attempts to clarify the nature and timing of information needs and sets the stage for a continuing and effective communication process.

Early in the evaluation planning process, then, and here at the point of specifically planning for effective communication, you must identify both those likely to have the greatest interest in the evaluation results and what that interest might be. Be aware, though, that you probably will find more people with interest than time, energy, and resources to serve those interests effectively. A useful distinction to keep in mind when identifying the audiences for your work is that between *primary users* and *secondary users.* Primary users are those specific individuals whose information needs you are commissioned to serve. The evaluation sponsor and/or those who request the evaluation are obvious primary users. Such individuals could represent a board of directors, a chief executive officer, a program director, a funding agent, or other program decision makers or policymakers. Primary users also may include key program staff or others who have direct, vested interests in a program. The lion's share of your reporting and communication energy should be directed toward these primary users. These are the individuals you most want to use your results; these individuals represent your chief audience.

Secondary users or audiences are other individuals or groups who may be affiliated with the program in some way and have an interest in the program and its evaluation. You may want to confer with these individuals as you develop your plans, you may want to incorporate their interests and perspectives in your data collection and you may well want to disseminate your results to them; but these are not your primary clients. Community groups, staff, participants, other organizations interested in the program, legislators, special interest groups, and a range of others depending on your specific situation might be viewed as secondary users.

An evaluator's role and the audiences he or she serves vary with each and every assignment, but some similarities in responsibilities and expectations generally fall into two different categories. Most likely, your role will resemble one of the two following general types:

(1) Your evaluation task may characterize you as a *helper* and *advisor* to the program planners and developers. During the early stages of the program's operation, you may be called on to describe and monitor program activities, periodically test for progress in achievement or attitude change, look out for potential problems, and identify areas where the program needs improvement. In this situation, you function as a troubleshooter and problem solver whose overall task is sometimes not well defined. You may or may not be required to produce a final written report at the end of your activities. An important part of your role, however, is the ongoing verbal and/or written feedback to the program's developers, managers, and/or staff as you discover information about the program's implementation, effects, and accomplishments. If this somewhat loosely defined job role seems close to the expectations for your present assignment, then you are most likely acting as a *formative evaluator.*

(2) You may have the responsibility for producing a *summary statement* about the general effects and accomplishments of a given program. In this case, you will most likely be preparing a final written summary report to be presented to the program policymakers and/or managers (e.g., funding agency, a corporate manager, district or state officials, legislators). You may be expected to describe the program, to produce a

statement concerning achievement of the program's announced goals, to note unanticipated outcomes, and possibly to make comparisons with an alternative program. While the bulk of your work may entail composing the written final report, your findings should be communicated on an informal basis throughout the course of the evaluation. If this role seems close to the expectations for your present assignment, then you are most likely acting as a *summative evaluator*.

In addition to the distinctions between formative and summative roles, there is also the related factor of whether you are carrying out your responsibilities as an *internal* or as an *external* evaluator. An internal evaluator is someone who is already an employee or associate of the organization or program being evaluated. If you are an internal evaluator, then you probably are already familiar with the personnel associated with the program, and with the goals of the program. This familiarity can greatly simplify your initial communication tasks if you have established working relationships with key personnel and with your primary users. However, an internal evaluator may face some disadvantages as well if previously existing relationships have not been productive or cordial.

An external evaluator, on the other hand, is someone who has no particular vested interest in the program or organization. Often hired as the result of a bidding process, external evaluators may not be familiar with the staff and their interrelationships or with the other potential users, even though the evaluation sponsors may know the evaluator personally or through previous work. An important first communication task for an external evaluator is to identify the key program personnel and primary users and to begin developing good working relationships with them. Such relationships may well be crucial in helping to reinforce the credibility, trustworthiness, and, in turn, utility and impact of the evaluation.

With your own relationship to the program clarified, you can begin to develop communication plans. Understanding your primary audiences and their needs is a critically important consideration in developing effective plans.

Understanding Your Primary Users and Audiences

Know your audiences

Most evaluations have many audiences to use or persons in a position simply to have an interest in evaluation results. None of these potential users should be ignored during the planning and reporting processes. Neglecting to correctly identify one or more of the primary users is a common mistake, one which can have serious repercussions. For example:

> At the request of the city council in a small community, an evaluator is contracted to conduct an evaluation of a drug abuse prevention program sponsored by the local police department for secondary schools. Without consulting with the police involved in the program, the evaluator proceeds to design the evaluation and to report information requested by the council members. When the evaluator finally delivers the results of the evaluation at a city council meeting, the police voice vehement opposition to her recommendations that certain activities in the program be eliminated and others expanded, saying that they had no voice in planning the evaluation. It does not reflect their priorities, they say, and they are reluctant to support its recommendations. By overlooking a group of primary users at a critical planning stage and undervaluing their importance as evaluation users, the group probably most likely in a position to gain something from the evaluation has been alienated.

An evaluator also may identify an audience that is too broad. Perhaps, for instance, you have presented a final report to a program planning committee—certainly primary users of the information. But you did not give special consideration to the committee chairperson, an individual with long-standing experience and influence within the committee and a respected opinion leader of the group. Without her support, no action is taken. A wiser approach would have been to meet individually with the chairperson to review your findings and to discuss their implications well in advance of the general committee meeting. This action would acknowledge her status within the group and would alert both you and the chairperson to potentially controversial findings before they are generally distributed.

Identifying your actual audiences—sometimes in spite of official pronouncements—is critical if you hope that your findings will be used. To a significant extent your credibility and the credibility of your findings rest on whether or not you have identified and incorporated primary users in your evaluation plan.

Find out what information the users need and why they need it

Produce a list of what people want to know and why they want to know it. To be effective, reports must be tailored to the *real problems perceived by administrators and practitioners.* Again, your credibility and the credibility of your findings are enhanced if you accurately identify or at least acknowledge the major issues confronting program personnel.

Before you even begin collecting data, and certainly before you attack a final report, find out what the decision makers consider to be acceptable criteria for program success. This may or may not coincide with your criteria for success; but in the end, the decision will be theirs and you must use criteria which they find credible. In the users' terms, at what level is the program expected to succeed? You might ask them quite directly, "Will this tell you what you want to know?" With this focus, you will be in a much stronger position to interpret and to present the findings in a way that is most relevant and credible to users.

For a variety of reasons, this all sounds much easier than it is in practice:

- *Different users want different information—even to answer the same question.* A funding agency may accept only valid and reliable test data to prove that a staff training program has been effective, while the personnel participating in the training program would find anecdotal reports and responses from interviews or questionnaires to be the most valid and believable evidence of program effects. Other audiences might require both kinds of information.

- *Some users do not know what they need.* In programs where evaluations are mandated by legal requirements, for example, evaluation clients or program staff may see the assessment simply as a trial to be endured, not necessarily as a process that will lead to useful information and enlightened decisions. If the users are not willing to commit to some criteria for measuring success before the evaluation starts, it is highly unlikely that they will accept or use your final recommendations. Formative evaluators consistently face the task of helping clients define not only program objectives, but also specific evaluation information needs.

- *Some users expect the evaluation to support a specific point of view.* They have already made up their minds about the strengths and weaknesses of the program, and they expect that the evaluation will only confirm their opinions. The results of the evaluation may very well *not* support their preconceptions. So it is vital that the evaluator identify the opinions early on so that he or she can anticipate potential controversies and design reporting procedures which take them into account. Alerting users to your finding discrepancies between their assumptions and the findings as they emerge rather than solely in a final report will make the users more receptive. In fact, an effective evaluation report will contain no surprises, especially with respect to central issues. All of the major questions will have been discussed with program personnel and decision makers from the very beginning, well *before* the final reporting stage. If the evaluation does not bring these issues to light early, the evaluator loses credibility.

• *For some users, the information needs change during the course of the evaluation.* It is not at all uncommon when a formative evaluation is well under way, for the users to identify new information they would like to have. Some trainers, for example, might mention that the computer operators in a pilot training program seem to be learning a new data processing system, but the operators have developed a strong dislike for the system. You might change your evaluation plans to include some attitude measures. Although you cannot constantly alter evaluation plans, try to reserve some small portion of your resources to meet requirements for unexpected information that crops up during program implementation.

If you want the users to listen carefully when you begin circulating your findings, you will have to pay attention to what they want to know. For example, a state director of youth services has been promoting a project to increase the number of permanent homes for foster children. He wants to know whether or not the project has encouraged foster parents to keep children on a permanent basis. As a major part of a final report, the evaluator discusses the rate of delinquency among adopted children and foster children. Drumming his fingers, the director cannot see how this information relates to the project's success, "So what?" he asks. "Are more foster parents keeping children longer as a result of this program or not?!"

Be careful to avoid giving decision makers almost but not quite what they need to know. For example, a federal agency administrator might need to know how many members of his staff will voluntarily agree to participate in a drug use test when a new drug screening program goes into effect. In this case, you cannot simply deliver information about the number of staff members who *endorse* drug testing. Endorsing testing is not quite the same as volunteering to be tested oneself.

Try to understand the user's viewpoint

If you intend to influence an audience, know its motivations and its idiosyncrasies, and cast your reporting plans accordingly. Choose a reporting form and style which takes their viewpoint into consideration, and anticipate the kinds of situations that will trigger negative reactions to your report.

Teachers, for example, work under rigid time constraints. They frequently complain (with some justification) about being required to attend meetings about topics of little immediate importance to them. Unfortunately, evaluation reporting sessions often fall into this category. In addition, many teachers have developed negative attitudes toward almost any decisions made at "the central office" by "all those desk jockeys up there who have nothing better to do than dream up more paperwork for us." If you plan to report evaluation information to individuals who hold attitudes such as these, adjust your reporting strategies to accommodate their attitudes. Some of the following actions might work well:

Attitude	*Reporting Accommodations*
I don't want to go to a meeting that wastes my time.	* Distribute information in an attractive, efficient memo or brochure. * Post the information on a centrally located bulletin board. * Report the findings quickly during a regularly scheduled staff meeting. * Meet with one person per division and let those individuals report to the others in their unit. * Ask the administrators or staff to decide on the most convenient time for a meeting.
I don't like the central office.	* Have local unit administrators present the information to their colleagues. * Have an administrator and a staff person present the findings jointly.

Through your personal manner and reporting plan, show that you are aware of the implications the findings have on the audience's lives. Pay attention to what you wear and to your style of language. Dress as you expect your audience will dress, and speak their language. Take objections into account and discuss candidly any risks that the evaluation results might hold for them.

Submit the report in time to be useful

The timing of an evaluation report can be critically important if you intend the information to be used. Deliver the results to coincide with the decision-making framework. If information comes too early, it could lose its impact. If it arrives too late, it will be history and probably have no impact. Changes are more likely to occur soon after the evaluation is completed, when the program staff and administrators are still in a flexible and self-analytic frame of mind. Delivered six months after the evaluation has been completed, the staff will be barely able remember the evaluator's name, old routines will have settled in again, and a prime opportunity for change will have slipped away.

Perhaps, for example, you find that the staff of a community college financial aid office is displeased with a recently installed computerized data management system. They have discovered in the course of using it during fall semester that the graphics component of the program—a feature they first found very attractive—has turned out to be too complex to use. You include this outcome in your results and deliver the final report during the summer. In the meantime, based on the staff's earlier favorable ratings of the system and in line with district's spring purchasing deadlines, financial aid directors from five community colleges in the district ordered the expensive data system. With boxes of unsatisfactory computer software on the doorstep, your tardy evaluation report can only be an irritant.

At the same time, it is important that the evaluator not present information prematurely, before sufficient data have been collected to draw valid conclusions or before the users are prepared to hear or to act on the findings. Those who commission the evaluation should be kept informed of its progress. This can be accomplished with brief meetings, phone calls, or one-sheet summaries or charts included in a memo, depending on the client's preferences.

Ill-informed decisions may be unavoidable when decisions must be made during a crisis or in ad hoc situations. They *can* be avoided if you know, in advance, *who* will be deciding *what* and *when*.

The last recommendation brings with it another concern equally important to understanding your primary, and perhaps secondary, users and their needs: understanding the timing of their information requirements. To accomplish this, you will have to become acquainted with their expected planning and decision-making schedule, the nature of their decision-making process, and the decision-making cycles that are anticipated. This will enable you to formulate an optimal reporting plan that provides relevant information at the points at which it can be most useful. In establishing your sensitivity to your users' needs, you also will be setting the stage for a productive working relationship and

DESCRIPTION OF EVALUATION USERS

Name of Individual of Group	Relationship to the program	Primary areas of concern	Key dates in decision-making process	Personal characteristics and preferences	Required Reports (date and type)	Other Reports (date and type)

Figure 1. An instrument developed by Phyllis Jacobsen to compile information about potential users of the evaluation information and their reporting needs and preferences.

establishing a solid basis for good communication. An empathetic and knowledgeable evaluator who establishes good rapport with the sponsors and other primary users, who listens keenly, and who can accurately translate and clearly articulate their perceived needs is well on the way to building trust in the evaluation's findings and foundations for the findings' use.

Developing a Reporting Plan

Developing an effective communication plan, it should be clear, is a complex endeavor. There are many factors to keep in mind as you develop and organize your efforts. It is a good idea to keep an up-to-date chart describing your intended users, their interests, and proposed reporting mechanisms. The following suggestions are also illustrated in Figure 1:

- Make a list of your primary users, and if feasible the secondary users whom you would like to affect. You may want to record on this list the dates when you actually make contact with each. The chart can become a useful reminder of how long it has been since your last contact. (Staying in contact is important to encourage the use of your work.)
- Add to the list a thumbnail sketch of what you know about your desired users: their relationship to the program, any relevant personal characteristics, their particular interests in the evaluation, and their preference for communication forms and style.
- Draw up a master chart of all your evaluation activities, and carefully mark all required formal reporting deadlines.
- Consider other points in your evaluation process and in your users' action plans when you can provide relevant information. If resources permit, add to the chart any additional important reporting points. These might be memos, interim reports, meetings or any foreseeable occasions when you feel it would be important to communicate with program personnel.
- Using the information from the chart, organize a time line so that you will keep track of important reporting dates. The time line should include all planned formal and informal reporting events, the key intended users for each, and the dates on which you actually complete the reports.

Chapter 2
Forms of Communicating Evaluation Findings

Once you are familiar with your primary evaluation audiences, with the dimensions of your evaluation role, and with the main questions which the study will address, it is time to consider *how* you will deliver your message. Communication is bidirectional. It flows between both the evaluator and those who are involved with the program. At the beginning of an assignment, the evaluator must try to *collect* as much information as possible from the funding agent, from agency people, program planners and staff, and from any other potential users. As the evaluation progresses, however, the communication flow begins to go the other way. The evaluator takes more of the responsibility for *providing* information.

Early in the planning stages, you pretty well decided who would receive information and when that information is needed. Now you must decide exactly how you will disseminate your findings. What forms of communication will be most effective? The following set of questions can serve as a guide for any message or form of delivery you choose. From the very outset, put yourself in the practitioner or user's place and ask the following questions:

(1) To what extent and in what specific ways is the information *relevant* to the user's real and compelling problems?
(2) To what extent is the information *practical* from the user's perspective?
(3) To what extent is the information *useful* and immediately applicable in the user's situation?
(4) What information will the user consider *credible* and what reporting practices will support that credibility?
(5) To what extent is the information *understandable* to primary users? In what ways might the reporting practices have to be adjusted so that the information is understandable to other audiences?

(6) How might reporting practices ensure that the information is delivered in a *timely* fashion so that it might be most useful?

Directly or indirectly, users apply these criteria to your reports, and they will accept or reject your information accordingly. The previous chapter recommended that you know your audiences and their needs well in advance. With this knowledge you can decide what kinds of information will be relevant and practical to them. But even this is not sufficient to facilitate use of your findings. This chapter offers some specific suggestions for designing reports which will be accessible, credible, and understandable as well. Such qualities will be affected directly by the communication media and styles you choose to employ. If your message is not believable or understandable, it goes without saying that it will not be usable.

There are any number of ways you can disseminate your findings. Unfortunately, too many evaluators fall back on the standard, but usually terminally dry, technical report form. It resembles a dissertation and sometimes reads like one. However, it is well to remember that the standard form is not the only choice available and certainly not the best alternative for all audiences and circumstances. Figure 2 lists eleven different potential audiences for your findings and suggests that those audiences do not all want the same information delivered the same way. Some audiences may have an interest in your results but no time to study them in detail. Others may have little knowledge about the program or about evaluation practices, so they would have difficulty understanding a technical report. Some audiences have only a potential or passing interest in the program—an interest that a dull report might kill. So take the time to *tailor the message* to the receiver, particularly if the receiver is a primary intended user of your evaluation.

As Figure 2 shows, primary users such as funding agencies, program administrators, and sometimes advisory committees and boards of trustees usually require the most technical and detailed messages. After all, they are paying the bills and making crucial decisions about the continuation of the program, and in their eyes your report must be as complete and as technically credible as possible. This is not to say that they will read a full report. Sometimes they do. But even if they do not, they usually will want to have the full set of findings available for easy reference.

Influential reports, even technical reports, often are short and to the point. Brevity and clarity are crucial. If technical reports are read at all,

POSSIBLE COMMUNICATION FORM

AUDIENCE/USERS	Technical Report	Executive Summary	Technical Professional Paper	Popular Article	News Release, Press Conference	Public Meeting	Media Appearance	Staff Workshop	Brochure, Poster	Memo	Personal Discussions
Funding agencies	X	X									X
Program administrators	X	X	X	X	X			X		X	X
Board members, trustees, other management staff			X	X							
Advisory committees	X	X	X								
Political bodies (city councils, legislatures)			X	X							
Community groups						X					
Current clients						X	X				
Potential clients											
Program service providers (teachers, technicians, etc.)	X		X					X	X	X	X
Organizations interested in program content				X	X						
Media					X	X					

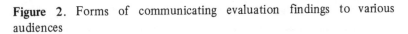

SOURCE: Adapted from Anderson and Ball (1980, pp. 102-103).

Figure 2. Forms of communicating evaluation findings to various audiences

they are usually scanned by administrative and legislative staff advisors, all very busy people. One legislative assistant suggested that to make evaluation information more useful to State Assembly members, the evaluator should "just write down the conclusions of your report in one sentence, in large type, in the middle of a single sheet of paper."

Perhaps the most important part of the final report is not the bulk of data and analyses. It is the *executive summary*, which may come at the beginning or at the end of a report. In a very few pages, sometimes accompanied by graphic displays or organized around straightforward questions, an executive summary outlines the major findings and recommendations of the study.

Other audiences may have an interest in your results as well, but they may not have the time, the vested interest, or the expertise to plow through all the technical details. They want to know the main points and how the findings might affect their lives or apply to immediate areas of interest. These users usually include community groups and program clients or potential clients. Program service providers, those who directly implement the program, probably also prefer a short, lay-person's version of the findings. On the other hand, service providers, with a naturally vested interest in the program and in its evaluation results, appreciate having access to a complete copy of the technical report. It goes without saying that the media prefer a concise written summary of findings—but written in a style fit to print in a newspaper or to report on television.

Tailor your message to your audience and to your evaluation role as well. It may be primarily as a formative evaluator, as a summative evaluator, or as some combination of both. Although each type of evaluator performs many of the same functions, there are some important distinctions in their reporting practices.

Formative Communication

If you are a *formative evaluator,* you maintain a fluid but constant relationship with the program during the course of its development and/or operation. Your reporting may affect important decisions about changes in the program during initial planning stages, when the program is installed, and when it is fully implemented. There are no hard and fast rules about formative reporting other than those agreed upon by the evaluator and the sponsor or funding agent when the evaluation assignment is negotiated. But there are some common practices.

In the first place, a formative evaluator reports to program planners and personnel who are familiar with the program rather than to distant funding people whose only source of knowledge about the program might be the final report. In many cases the formative evaluator is practically a program staff member—gathering opinions about preferred or more effective ways of installing the program, perhaps conducting short experiments to answer controversies that arise among the staff, and holding discussions to help the program planners achieve a comprehensive and rational statement of what the program is supposed to be doing. In this context, it is obvious that some findings are not intended for wide distribution. They may be confidential or they may not be of interest to anyone else outside the immediate program staff.

Exchanges of information between the evaluator and the practitioners can be frequent, formal (such as a scheduled meeting), or informal (such as a brief impromptu discussion in the hallway). Communication can take a broad range of forms: written reports, telephone calls, requests for clarification, reviews of preliminary report drafts, discussions over lunch, and so on. Frequent face-to-face communication between the evaluator and the program manager allows them to explore how the evaluation is going to date and what its ultimate findings might look like. The manager's anxieties are thereby reduced while the evaluator validates emerging impressions of the program.

In addition, the formative evaluator usually *monitors* the program, carefully describing the program that is occurring, making periodic assessments of performance, attitudes or other outcomes, or gauging the adequacy of the original plans as they unfold in real-world settings. Monitoring activities might require the evaluator to present periodic formal reports either orally to a group or in written form.

Considering the importance of face-to-face communication and of informal conversational exchanges of information about the evaluation between the evaluator and staff members, it is essential that the evaluator possess the necessary interpersonal skills to be able to communicate effectively. Some of these skills are *tact*, a personal quality resulting from experience working with people; *easy temperament; ability to listen;* and *genuine concern* and *caring.* Many psychologists and communications experts have written "how to" books on these topics. Among the guidelines they suggest are the following:

- Practice active listening.
- Focus feedback on sharing ideas and information rather than giving advice.
- Convey to your audience that you are seeing things from their point of view.
- Encourage open discussions of alternatives.
- Build on shared experiences and common values.
- Exhibit positive attitudes, such as

  - belief that differences of opinion are helpful,
  - belief that other party is a helpful resource,
  - belief in the trustworthiness of others.

- Be sensitive to the feelings and sentiments of your audience.

Consider exploring in detail some of these texts if you doubt your interpersonal skills.

It is important, above all, that the evaluator *be available* to program staff when they feel the need to communicate. Often, their questions will have some urgency which, if not satisfied, will result in diminished credibility for the evaluator, and for the value of the evaluation itself.

In addition to the usual informal communication activities (meetings, conversations, discussions), you also will want to consider a range of more formal options. In any event, you will want to consider the utility of several common forms of formative reporting: implementation reports, interim or progress reports, and technical reports. Any of these can constitute a written document, a formal oral presentation, or a meeting agenda.

Implementation reports.[1] Most programs prescribe that certain crucial events occur. For example, program participants should be selected according to certain criteria, particular materials and methods should be used, and activities should be completed by specific dates. Sometimes these important events do not occur at all. Sometimes they occur differently, possibly even better, than was originally planned. Sometimes they even occur smoothly as planned. In any case, program managers and planners need to know what is happening and whether the program or the original plans for it have to be modified. An implementation report provides this information.

In this type of reporting, a formative evaluator maps out and describes the activities and arrangements that have evolved, presenting findings either in writing or through discussions with project personnel. An implementation report should attend to such issues as these:

- Whether or not the program is being implemented as planned and as the audience expects. Do participants receive the materials and services that were proposed for them?
- What does a typical program experience look like?
- What effects have any changes had on the program—for example, have the attitudes of staff or participants changed?
- Are operations more or less efficient?
- What are the strengths and weaknesses of program operations?

Periodic formative evaluation reports might respond to the following questions:

- What should have occurred since the last report?
- What in fact has occurred?

- What are the reasons for the discrepancies, if any?
- What problems have occurred?
- What actions are recommended, if any?

Whatever their specific questions, periodic reports on program implementation must be *timely* so that corrective action can be taken before it
is too late to change.

Progress reports. Programs aim to achieve certain goals. While these
goals are hoped for or expected end products of the program, it is not
wise to wait until a program's end to assess the achievement of these
goals. An evaluator can regularly report progress toward the program's
general goals by indicating when specific objectives have been attained
or the extent to which program components have been completed.
Reports about progress can be *interpretive* as well as descriptive. That
is, they can include projections, based on current progress, of the
likelihood that a program will achieve its overall goals. Graphs can help
relate current results to eventual outcomes. For example, the trend
graph in Figure 3 illustrates that Group A is making better progress
toward the program goal than Group B. An accompanying list of which
objectives have not been mastered will encourage the staff to look for
"bugs" in the program and to plan changes.

Measuring and interpreting progress will be easier if the formative
evaluator has located or set up a control group. In these cases, both the
experimental and control groups can be regularly monitored and their
progress contrasted.

In general, the content of a progress report should address such
questions as these:

- What instruments were used to measure progress?
- Of what relevance and technical quality were these instruments?
- What progress has been made since the last report?
- Does this rate of progress indicate program success?
- What features of the program appear to promote or to hinder progress?
- What recommendations can be made for action, if any?

Technical reports on single issues. During a program's early stages, a
formative evaluator can conduct pilot studies, interviews, site visits, and
short experiments to answer questions about particular issues of
interest. For example, staff and management may have a difference of
opinion about the choice of procedures or program arrangements.
Would periodic mailings remind clients to attend the stress management
workshops? Or would the mailings simply add unnecessary costs?

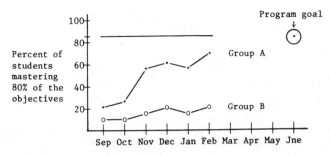

Figure 3. Progress of two groups of program students during a school year toward the overall goal of having 85% of the students master 80% (170) of the program's 212 objectives

Results of a small pilot study on one or two sample groups might help answer this kind of question. The findings could be disseminated to the program managers and the staff at a regular staff meeting or through a summary statement in a periodic report.

Summative Communication

More often than not, summative evaluators will find that their primary users will be the program funding agents and the program administrators, and that these audiences commonly expect a comprehensive final technical report at the end of the project. Such reports describe and justify the evaluation approach, the specific instruments and procedures used to enact it, and provide a comprehensive assessment of and recommendations for the entire program. The outline described in Chapter 4 of this volume will be of help as you build your report, or you may be required to follow a similar format required by the funding agency. If the report is to be submitted to a journal, use the journal's recommended outline. It probably will also be quite similar to the one in Chapter 4.

The summative report is nearly always *written* and detailed, so you should include as many charts and graphs as appropriate to deliver a clear, precise message. Chapter 3 explains how some of these visuals might be constructed. Visuals will also be helpful if you are called upon to deliver a condensed version of the final report to a public meeting or to the media. Good, clear charts and graphs translate well into informative transparencies, brochures, or poster illustrations to accompany an oral presentation. The funding agent may also require that accompanying materials be developed so that the lay public can understand the evaluation message.

Tips About the Evaluation Message

Whether your role is formative or summative, whether your communication is formal or not, these following few tips[2] will help heighten the impact and potential use of any kind of message:

Relate the information to necessary actions or decisions

If evaluation reports are to be seen as relevant, they need to indicate clearly the implications of the findings for people's work. Implications may seem obvious to you, but they may not be so obvious to the intended users. Do not force users to search through reports trying to tie findings and recommendations to their interests or to the decisions that have to be made. They most likely will not do it. If the evaluation was conducted to enlighten a decision or problem, then tie the findings directly to a statement of that decision or problem. One approach is to list each decision question to be addressed followed by summaries of the evaluation findings that relate to it; depending on your role and responsibility, you may also want to include *your* answer or recommendation for each question posed. This technique, illustrated in Figure 4, provides the busy reader with a quick summary.

Another technique which emphasizes an action orientation is to state implications in *cause-and-effect* or *if, then* terms (something true research reports rarely do). State simply and directly what the findings mean in terms of what actions should follow, what policy decisions should be made, or what will be the likely result of various alternatives. Recommendations usually suggest a single course of action. However, it might be more useful in some cases to provide alternative courses of action or options rather than single recommendations. A summary of data would be presented to explain the ramifications of each option.

You will want to be sure that such summary analyses include all the relevant information, and that your recommendations or suggested options—if you include them—are reasonable. One way of checking that the information you present is relevant is to have a group of program personnel, particularly those who might eventually use the material, review your initial findings. Not only can they provide a check on your clarity and interpretation but the process also enables you to add their practical perspective to the report.

Decision Question

Should the Extended Opportunity program at Y College hire additional part-time ESL tutors?

Information Summary

o Current level of service: Four E.O. funded tutors assist 40 ESL students who attend two individualized tutoring sessions per week. Tutors are working maximum allowable hours.

o Distribution of tutoring hours:

ENG A	40%	MATH 101	8%
ENG B	20%	ALGEBRA 10	15%
ENG 101	5%	ADVANCED MATH	12%

o Cost to the program: 80 hours at $4.00/hour, $320 per week or $1280 per month ($32 per student).

o Regular college tutoring program will not accept additional students.

Need:

o Y College testing service has identified 60 ESL students who also qualify for E.O.

o 70% of the E.O. students were surveyed to determine their satisfaction with available E.O. tutoring. The results:

There are _____ enough E.O. tutors to help me when I need it.

Always	Sometimes	Rarely	Never
20%	40%	30%	10%

There should be more tutors in _____

ENG A & B	ENG 101	MATH 101	ALG. 10/AdV. MATH
35%	30%	20%	15%

o Interviews with tutoring director and tutors indicated: They are working to capacity. An average of 5 students requesting help are turned away each day.

Figure 4. An example from an evaluation report of a format for relating evaluation information to an action which must be taken

Make the report credible

If people do not *trust* the results of the evaluation, it goes without saying that they will not use the information. In cases where findings are controversial, it is particularly important to attend to issues involving credibility. Technically accurate methodology can enhance credibility, but perhaps of equal or greater influence is the evaluator's style of interaction and reporting.

Methodologically, an evaluation is credible if data are collected in ways that the potential users perceive to be valid, reliable, and objective. Validity in this sense is not simply the technical validity of a scientific research study, but a validity that reflects organizational sensitivity. The evaluator must communicate a clear understanding of "what's going on" and how the organization "works" from the user's experience. A careful analysis of data from multiple sources adds to the evaluation's validity. Detailed accounts from qualitative studies, direct observations and interviews, indicate the evaluator's understanding of users' experiences and varied points of view. The report might also refer to the findings in other studies or to supporting statements from respected individuals. Credibility is enhanced if the evaluator specifies, explains, and justifies the methodology in terms which users can easily understand. At the same time, this reveals the evaluator's bias, if any, and any limitations the methodology might have. The key is to present a straightforward, well-rounded, knowledgeable, and complete rendering. Program strengths and weaknesses receive equal treatment.

Several volumes in this Kit offer specific suggestions about designing both qualitative and quantitative evaluations that are valid, reliable, and objective. Especially helpful would be *How to Design a Program Evaluation* (Volume 3), *How to Use Qualitative Methods in Evaluation* (Volume 4), and *How to Assess Program Implementation* (Volume 5).

An evaluator's style of personal interaction can improve credibility or destroy it. An active listener who is non-threatening and responsive is more credible than someone who maintains a cold aloofness and academic detachment—or worse yet, arrogance. This type of person hardly instills a sense of trust that he or she knows what life is really like for the practitioners. An evaluator should be supportive and educative, *explaining* the implications of findings.

The content as well as the style of a report should, as much as possible, resolve uncertainties about the issues under study rather than pass those uncertainties on to the users. Presumably, an evaluator was hired in the first place to reduce uncertainties. Give the most sound conclusions possible based on an explicit understanding of the strengths and weaknesses of the data.

Give the audience what it needs—and no more

If you expect your audience to absorb the information it most needs, do not confuse things by overwhelming the audience with other perhaps interesting but not necessarily vital information. If a project director asks you what a standard deviation means, do not make the mistake of covering the blackboard with statistical equations and graphs. If you give an audience too much, *all* of your information can become confusing.

Violating this rule is particularly easy when you must address a prestigious group—for example, a legislative hearing committee. You were probably taught early in life that people in authority should be told everything. Even if you were not, you have probably devoted a good chunk of your life to the evaluation project, fending off dangers to the evaluation plan and working long hours. You are eager, perhaps, to show the audience the clarity and brilliant complexity of the evaluation plan, the quick-thinking administrative maneuvers that saved the evaluation from disaster, or the mathematical genius so obviously guiding the analyses. DO NOT DO IT! You will bore the audience to death and render the findings indigestible.

**Present an attractive, evocative report that
matches the style of the audience**

There is no reason why an evaluation report must be dull—either dull sounding or dull looking. If your budget will allow, involve a graphics specialist in your reporting plans. The least a graphic artist can do is suggest designs for an impressive cover, taking into consideration the quality of paper and color that best fits the mood of your message and your audience. Graphics specialists may also be able to add clarity and punch to your charts and graphs. But they can do much more. If you are charged with disseminating information to a wider public, a graphic artist can help you design posters, brochures, and leaflets that broadcast an easily understood message.

Do not be afraid to use visual images as part of the overall data collection strategy. Photographs, videotapes, and film can be used to great advantage in some evaluation situations. They might illustrate the findings which emerge from other more conventional data collection methods. They might also be used to demonstrate the implementation of program elements or of outcomes. As with any other means of collecting data, visual images must also be valid, reliable, accurate, and must be interpreted in terms of the political ramifications of what they illustrate.

About the Written Medium

This section deals especially with *written* efforts to communicate evaluation information. The principles in this section apply to memos, news releases, and written communications other than formal evaluation reports. They can be applied, as well, to formal and informal oral presentations.

Start with the most important information

When reading for information, readers seek out the most important points first. Having learned these larger "truths," they then have a framework on which to hang the smaller, less significant pieces of the message. This principle underlines the familiar, yet vital, advice: "Tell them what you're going to tell them, then tell them, then tell them what you told them."

Evaluation reports which follow the standard outline sound like college dissertations. This loyalty to prespecified scientific formats stems partly, no doubt, from evaluators' desires to be accepted as genuine researchers. Although a dissertation outline has many merits, it does not provide readers with what they want to know *when* they want to know it.

David Ewing (1974, pp. 59-62) recommends that a piece of professional writing should meet five requirements:

(1) Does the opening paragraph or section specify the *subject matter* of the report, memorandum, letter, or other document?
(2) Does the opening telegraph the principal *message* that the writer will emphasize?
(3) If it is important to the reader to know *why* the document was written, is the reason made clear?
(4) If the report is lengthy or complex, does the opening section outline the *organizational scheme* to be followed?
(5) If the report were to be sent out with a covering letter for some reason, would you be able to forego summarizing in the letter the main ideas, conclusions, or recommendations of the report?

A good way to ensure conciseness is to *imagine that your reader will not have time to get through the whole report.* Pretend that some interruption may cause the report to be laid aside and perhaps never be looked at again. You have to say as much as possible right away!

Here are some more specific suggestions for providing the reader with easy access to the salient parts in the report:

- Put a clear abstract at the front.
- Make your evaluation findings the first chapter.
- Start *each* chapter, subsection, and paragraph of your report with the most important point to be made in that section. Put your diamonds right on top of the heap to be sure they will be seen by your readers.

Highlight the important points

Help your reader determine what facts are most important. Putting the most important information first is one way, but there are additional ways to do this:

(1) Use *descriptive section headings.* For example, the heading "Nurses' Attitudes" tells you less than "Nurses' Attitudes Toward the Program," which tells you less than "Nurses Favor the Program." Headings in a report serve the same function as headlines in a newspaper. Descriptive section headings can also spark interest and motivate the reader to read further. Interesting and informative headings will pull a reader through a report that would not otherwise be read to its conclusion.

(2) Write the first draft of your report using as many section headings as you can think of; then read it over and double the number of headings.

(3) Try using headings as a running commentary, parallel to the report text:

CLOVERDALE FIRST-GRADERS ON PAR WITH NATIONAL AVERAGE	The "average Cloverdale first-grader" comes to school only slightly less well-prepared to start his or her academic career than does the "average American first-grader." The districtwide prereading readiness score was at the 48th percentile.

(4) The *spacing and layout* of a report text can be used to highlight information. Consider this text:

The three areas of the district show rather different patterns of strengths and weaknesses on the subtests. For South Side and North Hills students, Math Concepts is the weakest subtest and Math Computation the strongest, with Reading in between.

For Central City students, on the other hand, all reading scores are higher than the math scores, and there is no difference between the two math subtests. North Hills students tend to score higher than South Side students in math, but about the same in reading.

Reformatting improves its readability:

Addition of an outline format with dots and more white space	The three areas of the district show some-what different patterns of strengths and weaknesses on the subtests: • For South Side and North Hills students, Math Concepts is the weakest subtest and Math

	Computation the strongest, with Reading in between.
	• For Central City students, on the other hand, all reading scores are higher than the math scores, and there is no difference between the two math subtests.
	• North Hills students tend to score higher than South Side students in math, but about the same in reading.
Boxes	For South Side and North Hills students, Math Concepts is the weakest subtest and Math Computation the strongest, with Reading in between.
Changes in typestyle	For *Central City* students, on the other hand, all reading scores are higher than the math scores, and there is no difference between the two math subtests.
Underlining	<u>North Hills</u> students tend to score higher than South Side students in math, but about the same in reading.
Capital letters	For SOUTH SIDE and NORTH HILLS students, Math Concepts is the weakest subtest and Math Computation the strongest, with reading in between.

Make your report readable

Whether your audience consists of professionals or laypeople, its members are busy people. You should therefore make the reading easy without sacrificing accuracy. Consider these pointers to help increase reading ease:

(1) Before you start to write, create an imaginary reader. For example, assume that this reader is a community member, someone who is *not* a professional in the program area. As you write, keep this person in mind.

(2) If you feel suitably uninhibited, dictate the first draft into a tape recorder. Again, imagine that you are explaining the various aspects of the program to an interested, but relatively uninformed individual.

(3) Once you have a draft, check the vocabulary to make sure you have used familiar words.

Instead of:	*Use:*
obfuscate	cloud
configuration	pattern
differential	gap
dichotomous cross-classification	2×2 table
utilize	use
facilitate	help

Jargon, a shorthand language that develops among specialists, is not easily understood by outsiders. Most jargon, while adding words to the language, does little to improve it. Ernest Boyer (1978), President of the Carnegie Foundation, once complained that a manuscript was too technical for release to the general public. When the criticism was voiced to a colleague, the reply was, "I guess we'll have to laymanize it"!

If you must use a technical term unfamiliar to readers, define it clearly. This may be done in a footnote, an aside, or as part of a glossary (if the report must contain *several* technical terms). The importance of defining words that are likely to be unfamiliar to your reader cannot be overemphasized.

(4) Use active verbs as much as possible. Generally, active verbs shorten sentences and increase their impact.

Example. *Passive* verb sentence: The scores of the patients in the program were higher than those of the patients in the control group. (19 words)

Active verb sentence: Patients in the program scored higher than patients in the control group. (12 words)

(5) Cut out the deadwood. As you edit your report, look for unnecessary words and phrases. Sometimes editing is best done by someone else. If you must do it yourself, allow a day or two to pass between when you write and when you edit.

(6) Shorten your sentences. Cutting out deadwood and using active verbs will shorten some of your sentences. Others that are still too long should be broken apart.

Example. The community advisory group held informative as well as entertaining monthly programs at different project sites during September through June, but did not meet in December. (26 words)

The community advisory group held informative and entertaining monthly meetings at different project sites. They met every month between September and June, except December. (24 words)

(7) Write shorter paragraphs. There is nothing so discouraging as looking at a solid wall of text. As you edit your material, try to convert these solid walls to shorter paragraphs. Ideas which require lengthy discussion, of course, are not easily broken down. But where you can confine paragraphs to a single idea, you will increase readers' understanding of the material and reduce the effort they must expend. Even one-sentence paragraphs can be very effective.

(8) Personalize your text. Try to make your text sound less like an insurance policy and more like a letter to a friend. Of course, you must judge

whether or not this tip is appropriate to your audience(s). Some audiences will respond well to a casual, personal approach; others will expect and want a formal document. Here are ways you can personalize the material:

Use first person pronouns. Until recently, the use of "I" and "we" in writing was considered improper. According to the current fashion, referring to yourself and your audience as "he" and "they" often sounds stilted and false.

Use contractions. Contractions in written text tend to make the material more natural. They're being used more and more in "formal" written material—even in annual reports for business and industry.

Use "shirt-sleeves" language. As you rack your brains for a way to say that a program component is headed for hard times unless changes are made immediately, consider saying it this way: "The program component is headed for hard times unless changes are made immediately." If your audience does not mind the informality, it will certainly understand your message. Ewing (1974) reports that phrases like "pull the rug out from under us" and "catcalls from the sidelines" have been found in technical reports to the President of the United States. Casual but expressive shirt-sleeves terms can be quite effective, but only *when used sparingly.*

About Verbal Presentation

Practicing evaluators have discovered a few principles to increase success when making verbal presentations to evaluation audiences. These are summarized below.

Make the presentation interesting and varied

A verbal presentation should have enough variety to keep the audience entertained. Only an awake audience can be expected to hear your message. Almost anything you can do to get and keep their attention is therefore warranted. The positive reception given to even slightly interesting evaluation presentations reflect the deadly, dull character that audiences expect such presentations to have.

Here are some techniques for adding interest to your oral reports:

(1) *Do something different.* This means something different from what the audience is used to. The lecture approach is the most common method of presentation. Audiences expecting a lecture will perk up at the appearance of half-a-dozen slides or transparencies. Some example of novel presentation formats include, but are certainly not limited to the following:

- Skits. Do not rule this out; skits can work well with many evaluation topics.
- Audiovisual shows with commentary
- Symposia or panel discussions involving the program's major actors
- Question and answer sessions

(2) *Vary the format.* Five minutes of lecture, four minutes of lecture with slides, one minute of slides with no commentary, four minutes of questions and answers, and one final minute of lecture summary—this scenario probably makes a more interesting showing than fifteen straight minutes of lecture only. You can provide variety in many ways. Visuals, for example, can include any or all of the following: numbers, quotations, cartoons and drawings, photographs, and graphs. Try having two or more presenters. Perhaps they could argue or present opposing interpretations of the evaluation report. For the sake of sheer movement, try shifting the focus of the presentation to different parts of the room.

Do what comes naturally

It is important that you deliver a smooth, practiced, confident presentation. While a little nervousness won't hurt anything, if you are too shaky, your audience's attention will focus on you and not your message. You will feel least nervous with the presentation style that is most natural to you, regardless of whatever else has been said in this chapter. Many people, for instance, find it easier to talk to groups when there is something else to do besides just talk, such as show visuals or operate equipment. Knowing people in the audience also helps to relieve stage fright. However, when you must give a presentation to strangers, find out something about them that will help you see them as similar to people you have successfully talked with in the past.

Practice can certainly improve your presentation. Perhaps some friends could critique your delivery. Complicated audiovisual presentations will need several dry runs with attention given to the arrangement of the equipment and the room. If you fear a question and answer session, have friends or colleagues ask you the most difficult questions they can think of and then critique your answers. A word of caution here: If you do begin with this kind of practice, you must continue it until you feel comfortable. A *little* practice can sometimes *increase* anxiety.

Make the visuals large and simple

Visuals which accompany verbal presentations must be large enough for the audience to see. You would be surprised how many speakers violate this rule. When designing a visual, find out where the person farthest from the visual will be sitting, and design the visual so that he or she can see it clearly. Charts full of numbers, unless they are very large (wall-size), are not effective with large groups, though they can be used with presentations to just a few people. Even then, though, the charts must be large enough so that people sitting several feet away can see them.

Do not make transparencies for the overhead projector from typed material unless you use a typewriter with very large type, perhaps a primary typewriter. You *can,* however, use typewritten copy—especially from a 10-pitch (pica) or a primary typewriter—to make slides. Remember not to put too many words on the slide; one to ten words is sufficient. Most slides used to support oral presentations contain too much information; the audience is not allowed sufficient time to think about what it is seeing. When presenting a slide or transparency, give the viewers a few moments to explore it before talking. They will examine it anyway and may be distracted from what you are saying.

Involve the audience in the presentation

Find a way to have your audience act or respond during the presentation. Learner involvement with the material is a basic teaching principle. Involving an audience can be as subtle as getting them to laugh at opening jokes or as overt as having them roleplay. You could, for example, ask teachers to roleplay presentation of your achievement test results to parents with whom they will be having conferences or staff to roleplay a presentation to their board.

Here are a few audience involvement techniques:

- Ask for a show of hands in answer to questions—for example, "How many of you have worked in schools?" This also helps you better identify your audience's background.
- Ask them to predict results before you present them.
- Ask members of the audience to group themselves into particular seating arrangements.
- Ask them to help interpret your results. You might even ask for suggestions about how to present your *written* report.
- Build audience activities into your presentation. For example, give out cards on which people can write questions to be answered after your formal presentation; or arrange for group discussions about sections of your report.
- Involve the audience with an advocacy-adversary approach. Divide the group into advocates, adversaries, and neutral positions. Each group reviews the report from its assigned perspective and contributes to a lively and balanced debate over the data and results.

- Ask the audience to take notes on the presentation instead of preparing handouts to be taken home. Or have them fill in blanks you have left in the handouts to emphasize what you want them to particularly notice.
- Test them on the material you have presented. This can be safely done more frequently than you think.
- Ask someone in the audience for help with the equipment.

One last tip: Do not apologize for involving an audience in your presentation. If you are apologetic or give the impression you are impinging on their rights, they may feel that indeed you are. People won't mind participating if you seem to know what you are doing.

About Difficult Audiences

Audiences may at one time or another be difficult—slow to comprehend, skeptical, or even hostile. Since standard methods of presentation are often inadequate in adversity, the following tips are offered.

Have a primary user present the content of the report to someone else

This principle, well applied, might consist of any of the following:

- having a director present, or co-present with you, the evaluation findings to staff members
- having the program director report the evaluation findings to the board of directors
- having program staff present the evaluation findings to interested community groups

You could, in fact, arrange that evaluation results be distributed from group to group along the official chain of command in the organization. For example, Figure 5 shows the flow of shared evaluation results within a school district. This arrangement forces each district staff member to look at the evaluation results at least twice: upon receiving them and when passing them on. This approach is only effective, of course, if information is delivered accurately at the lower levels. If you choose this approach, you will probably need to deliver training and monitor the communications system.

Have someone else deliver the information

Try to be realistic about when you can and cannot handle distributing evaluation results yourself. Perhaps you

- lack direct access to the audience,

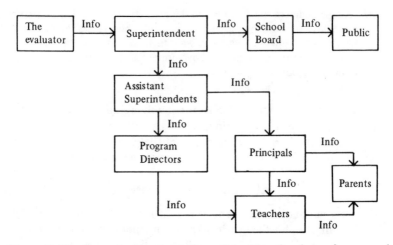

Figure 5. The flow of evaluation information along the chain of command in a school district

- are short on skills needed to get across the information effectively (for example, maybe you have stage fright), or
- are immersed in a personality or ideological conflict with members of the audience.

In such situations, find someone without these disadvantages to deliver the information. Remember, your main objective is to get the audience to understand and use the evaluation information.

Reinforce, reinforce, reinforce

A common problem with reporting evaluation information is that the audience usually hears it only once. To be properly absorbed, it should be heard more often than that. It should be reinforced. You cannot, after all, blame audiences for not using evaluation information if they never understood it. You can get audiences to attend more than once to your report by following many of the suggestions presented in this chapter. For example, if you are going to distribute new evaluation information to potential users, you would be wise to include in your reporting strategy one or all of the following practices:

- Submit a rough draft of the report to the primary user(s) for editing or review.
- Release a brief summary of the final report to the primary user(s).
- Discuss the report privately with individual users.

- Make a verbal presentation of a summary of the findings with visuals to the audience who will read the written report.
- At the direction of the primary user or evaluation sponsor, tell reporters about the findings so the audience reads about it in local newspapers.
- Bring up the findings in conversations on other topics with appropriate people, and relate the findings to actions being discussed.
- Have one audience present the information to other audiences.

About Working with the Press

This section gives some advice about making reporters' jobs easier and ushering your evaluation through the public media so that it is reported accurately. Note that some of these suggestions could be applied to any audience.

Train reporters

Most reporters have not had sufficient training to easily understand statistical evaluation studies. Their generally high intelligence coupled with native curiosity, though, makes them good and grateful recipients of in-service training. You can educate reporters by means of formal workshops or one-to-one discussions.

Formal training workshops should not be propaganda sessions. They should deal strictly with concepts the reporters need to understand to easily and correctly interpret the sorts of evaluation information you distribute. These sessions will be better attended and more effective if they are held just prior to the release of some important information. You might even go so far as to hold a training session for reporters during the hour or so before the press conference begins. Consider, for instance, the value of discussing, immediately prior to releasing standardized test scores, such topics as these:

- What are percentile scores?
- How are percentile scores derived?
- What is wrong with the statement, "All children should be able to read at this grade level"?
- What are some well-known correlates of achievement test scores or of other outcomes you are investigating?

When you consider the number of people, including practitioners, policymakers, and the lay public, who get their information from newspapers, radio, and television, you realize how much confusion can be avoided by an information workshop with key media representatives.

Take advantage, as well, of every opportunity you find to give one-to-one training. Reporters who want a story badly generally will listen to anything in order to get it. Interviews, then, can be a fruitful setting for some teaching by you and learning by them. Assume, when being interviewed, that the reporter knows nothing about the topic you are discussing. Explain your jargon, and give mini-courses on such things as these:

- the benefits and difficulties of random assignment of subjects to control groups
- significance tests—what they mean
- criterion- and norm-referenced tests—their benefits and limitations
- the use of triangulation in qualitative designs

You may see the results of these conversations reflected in clearer news articles or feature articles about non-crisis, non-sensational aspects of evaluation. The best benefit these discussions can have is development of mutual respect between you and the press. Cooperative relations can only improve the accuracy and thoroughness of the evaluation news that the public receives.

Write news releases

Misquoting by reporters is common, usually because a reporter did not record the comment correctly in the first place or because he or she did not have time to write it down and was forced to reconstruct the comment from memory. You can guard against this situation by writing *news releases* and giving them to reporters before a press conference or interview. News releases should be clear, to-the-point, and comprehensive. Well-written news releases will cause a reporter's "quote-accuracy index" to go up and your blood pressure to come down.

News releases should follow most of the rules presented above under "About the Written Medium." The best tip to remember is to put the most important information at the beginning of the article. *Quotations* are good ways to draw attention to the most important points within a news release. For example:

Dr. John Jefferson said today, "We are pleased and excited about Program X's effectiveness. An evaluation study shows that the recidivism rate among drug abusers in Project X is lower than among those not in the program."

A news release should include the name, address, and phone numbers—work and home—of the person who should be contacted in case of confusion or if the reporter needs more information. If the news must be published on a certain day or will be outdated after a certain time, this should also be prominently mentioned. The news release should close with the marks ### to let the reporter or editor know that he has come to the end of the news release, not just the bottom of the first page.

Your organization's public relations officer may be the appropriate person to send out the news release. Be sure to check policy before doing this on your own. Figure 6 is an example of a news release.

Be honest with reporters

You must consciously strive to achieve a reputation for credibility and straightforwardness with all your audiences. A person whose job is to collect and share information cannot be caught dissembling or lying. This is particularly true when talking to reporters. Answer reporters' questions honestly. If you cannot do so, tell them clearly why you cannot. For example:

> The CEO and the board of directors are studying the report right now. It would be a violation of my contract with them to discuss the report with the press before they have had a chance to review it. The program administrator will release the report to the public and the press in a week. I will be glad to answer any questions that you might have then.

Such candor will be accepted, even if reluctantly.

Many times reporters ask seemingly simple questions to which they want simple answers: "Why is the rate of violent crime higher in minority communities than in white areas?" or "Why isn't Program X succeeding?" Your immediate desire might be to preface answers to these questions with hours of background. If possible, condense those hours of explanation into a five-minute summary. Your summary should give the reporter some feel for the complexity of the situation. If the question is one to which you do not know the answer or if you are not familiar with the research in the area, do not bluff. You are likely to find your weak generalities printed on page one of the local paper.

You must accept that reporters are talking to you for only one reason—to get a story. To write a story that sells, they must ask hard questions. Their who, what, where, and when questions are easy to answer—they are the same questions you answered in the evaluation:

- *Whom* is the program serving?
- *What* are the program effects?

```
                            NEWS RELEASE

Contact:  Dr. Ruth Pitts                              May 2, 1988
          Director, Research & Evaluation             (Release on
          Passell School District                     May 5, 1988)
          145 Oak Avenue
          Passell, Texas

Phone #:  (512) 413-1045 (work)
          (512) 825-4711 (home)


  "Passell students scored higher this year on their annual achievement
tests than they did last year."  Superintendent John Jefferson made this
announcement in a special news conference.

  High school and Junior high students scored an average of two to three
percentile points higher than last year, and elementary students scored
three to five percentile points higher.

  "We can't be sure exactly why our students are doing better," Jefferson
said.  "But we think that the increase is related to the changes we have
made in our reading and math courses."

  For the past year, teachers and curriculum specialists in the district
have been revising the math and reading courses.  These revisions were
requested by the School Board in April, 1987, in response to parents'
concerns about reading and math achievement.

  Jefferson offered another explanation for the improved scores.  "During
the last few years, students and teachers may not have been taking the
test as seriously as we think it deserves to be taken.  This year, however,
attendance on the test days was higher than it's been during the past five
years," he said.

  Dr. Ruth Pitts, director of research for the district, added, "Our
research staff monitored the testing.  We made unannounced visits to five
percent of the classes when the testing occurred and found that correct
testing procedures were followed closely".

  Students will receive their individual scores at the end of May in
brochures that explain the scores.  Students are being asked to take the
brochures home to their parents.

  The tests were given to students during the middle of April.  High school
students took the Sequential Tests of Educational Progress (reading, math,
science, and social studies).  Elementary and junior high students took the
California Achievement Tests (reading and mathematics).
                              # # #
```

Figure 6. Example of a news release

Reporters will insistently ask *why* questions. These, of course, will likely have complex answers. In response to all their questions, easy or hard, you must give honest answers phrased in a way that the reporters understand.

In summary, this is what being honest with reporters means:

- being open and honest when responding to questions
- trying not to mislead them with a simplistic description of a complex situation
- refusing to bluff reporters or fake answers to their questions—doing this can backfire disastrously

Notes

1. For a more detailed description of what to include in a formative report about program implementation, see *How to Assess Program Implementation*, Volume 5 of the *Program Evaluation Kit*.

2. Many of the tips in this chapter were contributed by two practicing evaluators, Ann Moore Lee and Freda M. Holley.

References

Boyer, E. (1978). Cited by George Neill in "Washington Report." *Phi Delta Kappan, 59*(7).

Ewing, D. W. (1974) *Writing for results in business, government, and the professions.* New York: John Wiley.

Chapter 3
Using Tables and Graphs to Present Data

This chapter offers suggestions in the presentation of traditional tables and figures. Properly constructed and described, tables and figures not only convey major data summaries for a variety of written evaluation reports, they also provide the basic visual dimension for other forms of presentations. In addition to the traditional written report, results of evaluations might be shared through posters, brochures, overhead transparencies, and slide and/or tape presentations. A useful approach to preparing evaluation reports is to construct tables and graphs first. Resources permitting, it is also a good idea to involve a graphic designer at the early stages of evaluation planning to consider the role of graphic display in the overall reporting process.

Begin by compiling all your summarized data—descriptions of the program, data summary sheets for questionnaires and interviews, computer analyses, and so forth. Then, for each evaluation question you have chosen to answer, find the set of graphs and/or tables that you think will most effectively portray what you have found. Some evaluation designs and certain types of measurement instruments lend themselves almost exclusively to one type of graphic or tabular presentation. In the case of, say, objectives-based tests or true control group evaluation designs, then, some of the graphs in your report will have been determined for you.[1]

Once you have roughed out your graphs and tables, you can organize a report around them, arranging them in a logical order and writing supporting text to explain each one. In some cases, this may be all you need for the basis of a brief interim report to the program manager or staff. The summary could provide the basis for discussion about the progress of the program or about the progress of the evaluation itself. If instead you are planning a final report, consider taking the early draft with graphic summaries to the graphic designer.

When in doubt about whether you should use tables or graphs to summarize results, you are strongly advised to choose *graphs* or other pictorial displays. When they are correctly constructed, graphs make data clear and draw attention to important results. People leafing through an evaluation report generally pause longest to examine graphs. Not only can graphs clearly convey information, they also help the evaluator explore and analyze information, looking for trends to help interpret what happened.

The following pages describe various kinds of tabular and graphic data displays. Before you begin graphing, charting, and displaying, however, remind yourself of an important axiom: You can expect that some of your readers will look only at the graphs and tables in your report without reading the surrounding text. Because of this, every graph and table should be self-explanatory. This requires a complete title, full labeling, a key to symbols, and footnotes with commentary about, for instance, missing data or statistical significance. On the other hand, not everyone can read tables and graphs; some people will rely on the text. The text too, therefore, should describe and discuss at least the key results presented in the visuals, mentioning the important numbers—means, correlation coefficients, and the like.

Tables

Everyone knows what a table is, and you need little instruction about how to construct one. But to save you the trouble of having to invent usable formats, and to introduce a few customary practices accompanying the use of tables, this section describes some which commonly appear in evaluation reports.

Tables dealing with program implementation

If it is possible to describe the various components of a program succinctly enough to list them, then tables based on the list can be used to describe the program, show the results of its formative monitoring, and report summative evaluations of the nature of its implementation.

Table 1 shows a simple format for describing the principal features of a school program. When a program has a few distinguishing features, such a table could appear in the "Program Description" segment of a report (see Chapter 4, Section II.D). Programs with long lists of activities and materials will make it necessary to place the tables in an appendix.

If a program's features either were not specified in advance or if the program deviated widely from what was planned, the evaluator may have to describe the program's ultimate form. In this case, of course, Table 1 might appear in the "Results" section of a final report.

Notice that the caption describing a table always appears *above* it, with the word "table" completely capitalized. The first letter of each important word in the caption is capitalized as well.

An interim formative report about how faithfully the program's *actual* implementation conforms to the formal plan or about the staff's progress in carrying out activities on schedule might include tables similar to Table 2. A formative evaluator can use this table to report the results of monthly site visits to both the program director and the staff at each location. Each interim report consists of a table, plus brief but complete explanations of the ratings. In particular, one should explain why ratings of "N" ("needs attention") have been assigned to particular aspects of implementation.

Table 2 can be modified for summative reports by assigning an overall letter or number grade to the program or to each site, showing how adequately or accurately each program component has been implemented. This table would simply list each component and its assigned rating. Accompanying narrative would explain how the rating or index was determined.

Tables describing the evaluation

A table is a concise way of giving the audience an overview of the activities the evaluator has undertaken or completed—the tests given, observations made, reports delivered. A display such as Table 3 summarizes your data collection and reporting plans per objective.

Allotment of time to various evaluation tasks is displayed by a task time line, such as Table 4. A time line might also be useful for showing *program implementation,* particularly if the program is to be in segments or phases or if certain activities are to be confined to specific time periods.

Tables showing attrition

Tables such as 5 and 6 usually are the first to appear in the "Results" section of a final report.

Tables for displaying results from pre- and posttests and from time-series measures

Table 7 shows that tests have been administered to two groups—an experimental (E) group and a control (C) group. Table 7, and those that follow, appear in the "Results" section of the report. SD means standard

TABLE 1
Program Ex-Cell Implementation Description

Person responsible for implementation	Target group	Activity	Materials	Organization for activity	Frequency/ duration	Amount of progress expected
Teacher	Students	Vocabulary drill and games	SMA word cards, 3rd & 4th level	Small groups (based on CTBA vocabulary score)	Daily, 15-20 minutes	Completion of SMA, Level 4, by all students
			Teacher-developed word cards, vocabulary			None specified
			Old Maid			None specified
Teacher/Aide	Students	Language experience activities --keeping a diary, writing stories	Student notebooks, primary and elite typewriters	Individual	Productions checked weekly (Fridays); students work at self-selected pace	Completion of at least one 20-page notebook by each child; 80% of students judged by teacher or aide as "making progress"
Reading specialist/ teacher, student tutors	Students	Peer tutoring within class, in readers and workbooks	United States Book Company Urban Children reading series and workbooks	Student tutoring dyads	Monday through Thursday, 20-30 minutes	Completion of 1+ grade levels by 80% of students
Principal and teacher	Parents	Outreach--inform parents of progress; encourage at-home work in Urban Children texts; hold two Parents' nights; periodic conferences	One-sheet leaflet	All parents for program come to Parents' Night; other contact with parents on individual basis	Two Parents' Nights--Nov. and Mar.; 3 written progress reports in Dec., Apr., June; other contact with parents ad·hoc	Attendance by at least 50% of parents Contact with at least 80% of parents

TABLE 2
Project Monitoring

Objective 6: By March 1, 19YY, each participating clinic will select staff and review both staff and client needs to improve the delivery of primary health care to rural counties.

Winona County Health Clinic

Activities for this objective	Sep	Oct	Nov	Dec	Jan	Feb	Mar	Apr	May	Jun
		19XX					19YY			
6.1 Identify staff to participate		I	C							
6.2 Selected staff members review ideas, goals, and objectives		I	P	P	C					
6.3 Identify client needs		N	I	P	C					
6.4 Identify staff needs		N	I	P	C					
6.5 Evaluate data collected in 6.3 - 6.4						I	N	C		
6.6 Identify and prioritize specific outcome goals and objectives			I	N	P	P	C			
6.7 Identify existing policies, procedures, and laws dealing with outpatient health care delivery		N	I	P	P	C				

Evaluator's Periodic Progress Rating:
I = Activity Initiated   P = Satisfactory Progress
C = Activity Completed   N = Needs Attention

deviation. The column at the far right under both *Pretest* and *Posttest* shows the value computed by a statistical test to determine the significance of the difference—a t-test in this case. The asterisk identifies significant results and footnotes their level of significance.

Scores reported for the same group at six different times are shown on Table 8, which illustrates a display of data for a time-series evaluation design. You might also want to include the standard deviation for each measure to illustrate the spread of scores from one testing or observation to the next.

Tables for displaying test scores
from a single group, before-and-after
evaluation design

Table 9, by the way, has a footnote which uses the letter *a*. It is standard practice to show footnotes alphabetically in tables, saving asterisks for indicating statistical significance.

TABLE 3
Evaluation Data Collection and Reporting Plan
WASHOE Bicultural-Bilingual Program

Program Objectives	Population/Site Sampled	Type of Data	Collection Dates	Reporting Method and Date
(1) Second and third grade students participating in the bilingual-bicultural program will have a mean score of 20 or higher on the Rose-Smith Test of Cultural Similarities and Differences	2 classrooms at each site, randomly selected (only classes participating in program)	Rose-Smith Test of Awareness of Cultural Similarities and Differences	Pre-9/28 Post-5/31	Interim report: 10/30 Final report: 6/30
(2) Staff involved in the bilingual-bicultural program will develop and implement activities which encourage the expression and the appreciation of multicultural values in their classrooms	2 teachers per site	staff interviews	8/10	Interim reports: curriculum develop: 10/1
	5 students per site (culturally diverse)	student interviews	9/10, 1/10, 4/10	implementation: 11/1, 2/1, 5/1
	2 classrooms per site for 3 days	review curriculum materials produced.		Final report: 6/30
	Multicultural fair and school assembly	observe staff curriculum and development sessions	8/5-8/15	
		classroom observations	9/10, 1/10, 4/10	
		special program observations (photos)	12/15, 5/1	

51

TABLE 4
Evaluation Timeline

Tasks/Activities	Time in Months 19XX J J A S O N D / 19YY J F M A M	Completion Date	Reports and Deliverables	Program Evaluator	Program Director	Clinic Staff	Clinic Administrators	Aides	Clerical Staff
Review/revision of program plan		July 31	Revised written plan	37	8	-	6	-	16
Discussion about method of formative feedback alternatives		Sept 15	None	16	7	24	6	-	-
Planning of implementation-monitoring activities		Sept 30	List of instruments; Schedules of clinic visits	60	10	24	-	-	2
Construction of implementation instruments		Oct 10	Completed instruments	60	5	12	-	-	16
First meeting with staff		Nov 1	None	9	15	24	2	20	-
First meeting with clinic administration		Nov 8	First interim report	22	20	-	-	-	30

Number of personnel work hours consumed

TOTAL PERSON HOURS

TABLE 5
Number of Students Dropped
from the Analysis for Various Reasons

Reason	Number droppped from Experimental Group (n=75)	Number dropped from Control Group (n=80)
Absent for posttest	6	5
Absent from school during the program	3	3
Removed from group at request of parent	1	0
Left school	4	1
Other reasons	0	2
Total number dropped	14	11

TABLE 6
Nurses Remaining After Three Stages
of In-Service Program

	Number of nurses who registered to attend work-shops	Number and % who completed all workshops	Number and % who completed course require- ments and re- ceived credit
Volunteers	80	73 (91%)	50 (63%)
Attendance required	96	69 (72%)	69 (72%)

Tables for presenting correlations

Correlation refers to the strength of the relationship between two measures. A high *positive* correlation means that people scoring high on one measure also score high on the other. A high *negative* correlation also shows a strong relationship but in the opposite direction. A zero correlation means that knowing a person's score on one measure does not educate your guess about that person's score on the other. Correlation is usually expressed by a *correlation coefficient,* a decimal between –1 and +1, calculated from the scores that a single group of people have produced on the two measures.

The *graph* for displaying a correlation is a familiar one. Its axes represent scores on the two instruments of interest. As in Figure 7, a straight line represents the approximate relationship apparent between the two sets of scores.

TABLE 7
Pre- and Posttest Results
for Experimental (E) and Control (C) Groups

			Pretest			Posttest	
	N	Mean	SD	t-test of difference between E- and C-group means	Mean	SD	t-test of difference between E- and C-group means
E-group	32	10	10	.90	90	9	5.1*
C-group	35	58	8		80	7	

*statistically significant at .05 level *p = .05

TABLE 8
Mean Scores of E-Group
on Attitude Scale

	Before Program			After Program		
	Jan	Feb	Mar	Apr	May	Jne
E-group mean	20	25	30	50	55	60

TABLE 9
Mean Pretest and Posttest Reading and Math Scores
for Schools in the XYZ Program

Group	n[a]	Pretest	Posttest	t-test for difference between pre- and posttest
		Reading		
School A	401	59.4	64.3	3.8*
School B	720	50.2	70.5	12.2*
School C	364	40.9	60.2	4.5*
		Math		
School A	461	63.2	70.1	2.4*
School B	726	58.4	71.2	3.1*
School C	362	32.9	33.4	0.8

a. Number present for both the pre- and posttests, and therefore the students on whose scores the t-test was calculated.
*p = .05

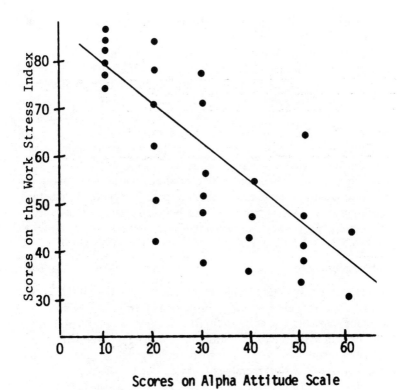

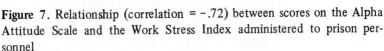

Figure 7. Relationship (correlation = −.72) between scores on the Alpha Attitude Scale and the Work Stress Index administered to prison personnel

At times you may need to report several correlation coefficients—the relationships, perhaps, among all the instruments you have administered during the evaluation. You might want to do this, for instance, to show that your findings from various measures present a consistent picture, strengthening your conclusions. You might, as well, want to present a case for the validity of one of your instruments by showing that its results are related or unrelated to some of the *other* measures given to the same people. The quantitative measures described on a correlation graph might be enhanced in the narrative report with information from qualitative measures. For example, Figure 7 illustrates a negative relationship between attitudes and work stress among prison guards. The Work Stress Index administered to the guards included a questionnaire with at least three open-ended questions about work conditions in the prison. Direct quotations taken from these responses will enliven the otherwise bland information portrayed by the graph. A few colorful descriptions or comments will bring a –.72 correlation to life.

You may want to illustrate relationships among a number of measures to show that people who score a certain way on one measure score predictably on one or more others. In any of these situations, you will want to construct a table of *correlations*.

Table 10, for example, contains a precise summary of a great deal of data on five measures. Besides students' mean scores on the various instruments, the table includes a correlation coefficient showing each measure's relationship to every other measure. The correlation between scores on the posttest and pretest is .76; between scores on the ability test and pretest, .38; between scores on the ability test and posttest, .49; and so on.

Tables containing symbols

Sometimes converting a table of numbers into *symbols* makes its message clearer, even though some details are lost. Table 11, for instance, presents a format useful for showing the proportion of staff members in state supported museums completing in-service training activities recommended by the state funding agency. The goal is to have at least half of the staff members complete each activity.

Using a performance standard, Table 12 translates the same data into symbols showing each museum's success or failure to meet overall program goals. Note how the title changes from table to table. The first words of the title usually refer to the numbers found in its body, but addition of symbols makes this difficult. Table 11 shows actual percentages of staff completing activities. Table 12 uses a criterion set at 50% of staff completing to show which museums meet program goals.

In the next section, which deals primarily with graphs, you will find a few additional examples of tables from which exemplary graphs have been constructed.

Graphs

Bar graphs

Bar graphs are common in evaluation and research reports—and for good reason. They are easy to understand. The data in Table 13 have been graphed to produce Figure 8. While examining Table 13 and Figure 8, take note of the following:

TABLE 10
Means, Standard Deviations, and Correlations
Among Measures Used for the Evaluation

	Measure	n	Mean	SD	Correlations 1	2	3	4
1	Pretest	55	13.5	6.1				
2	Posttest	55	23.1	12.9	.76*			
3	Ability test	55	18.9	6.5	.38*	.49*		
4	Effort rating	55	3.7	1.1	.42*	.50*	-.11	
5	Work done	55	25.1	17.8	.53*	.37*	.10	.27*

*p = .05

TABLE 11
Percentage of Museum Staff Completing
In-Service Training Activities

Museum	Number of Staff	Cataloguing Techniques	Display Construction	Community Rapport	Education Outreach
A	20	80	50	50	10
B	30	82	20	20	10
C	15	100	75	50	100
D	7	100	100	10	50

TABLE 12
In-Service Training Activities Completed
by 50% or More of the Staff in County Museums

Museum	Number of Staff	Cataloguing Techniques	Display Construction	Community Rapport	Education Outreach
A	20	+	+	+	-
B	30	+	-	-	-
C	15	+	+	+	+
D	7	+	+	-	+

Key: + = activity completed by 50% or more of the staff.
  − = activity completed by less than 50% of the staff.

(1) A graph is called a *figure* when labeled and referred to in text. The caption for a figure is placed *under* it, and only the word "figure" and the first word of the caption are capitalized.

(2) In both tables and graphs, the main comparisons of interest are kept adjacent. The principal aim in Table 13 and Figure 8, for instance, is to compare posttest scores of tutoring program participants with those of non-participants—not to compare older students with younger ones. Therefore, *age* is used as the *first* division, naming the major titles of the table and defining the horizontal axis of the graph. The *evaluator, then, can place indicators of participation* numbers in the table and bars in the graph—*close together.*

(3) A key is provided for the bar graph.

(4) To provide precise information, means per group are shown above the bars in the graph.

TABLE 13
Mean Posttest Scores of Children
Who Had or Had Not Participated
in the Cross-Age Tutoring Project

Group	n	Mean score[a]
Older children		
participants (tutors)	8	30.3
non-participants	14	15.8
Younger children		
participants (tutees)	24	18.1
non-participants	25	18.3

a. The highest mean score possible was 36

(5) Both the table and the figure indicate the number of cases, n, on which each mean is based.

Bar graphs are particularly useful for presenting data about the achievement of objectives. If the graph has been constructed so that each bar represents one objective, a quick glance can pick out the strengths and weaknesses of a program.

Table 14 presents the data from which Figure 9 was drawn. Notice how much easier it is to see the pattern of completion from the figure.

If a pretest and a posttest have been given as part of the evaluation plan, the scores from both can be shown on a graph. In Figure 10, pretest results are represented as white bars, and posttest results have been added as shaded bars. The difference between the heights of the white and shaded bars shows for which objectives there has been an increase in the number of students passing. Gains have been made mainly in objectives 5, 6, and 7.

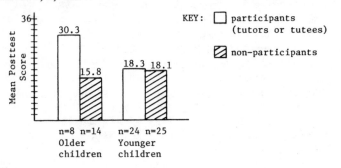

Figure 8. Mean posttest scores of children who had or had not participated in the cross-age tutoring project

TABLE 14
Percentage of Patients in Cardiac Stress
Reduction Program Achieving the 7
Objectives at the Completion of the Program (N = 30)

Group	Objective Number						
	1	2	3	4	5	6	7
Hospital A	91	76	33	13	7	56	2

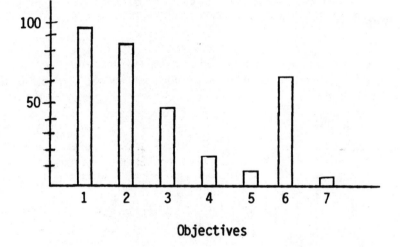

Objectives

Figure 9. Percentage of patients in the Cardiac Stress Reduction Program achieving the 7 objectives at the completion of the program

TABLE 15
Mean Percentage of Students in Program X
Achieving the 12 Objectives at Pretest and Posttest

Group	Objective #											
	1	2	3	4	5	6	7	8	9	10	11	12
Ninth grades (n=23)												
pretest	91	76	34	33	38	16	13	7	56	16	22	0
posttest	77	62	43	41	66	35	30	11	30	7	7	2

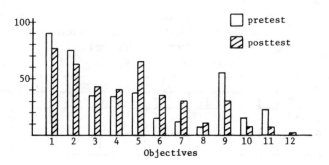

Figure 10. Mean percentage of students in Program X achieving the 12 objectives at pretest and posttest

A graph can also be used to display results from *two groups*—an experimental and a control group, as shown in Figure 11:

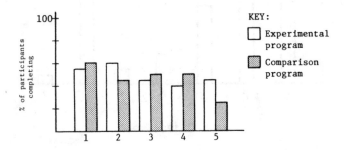

Figure 11. Final results of experimental and comparison groups completing 5 program objectives

Figure 12 shows a method for graphing results per objective when a general program *goal* prescribes a desirable criterion. For some objectives, the goal of a 100% completion may have been set. It might have been decided, for example, that *all* students should be able to read traffic signs accurately or know how to make change. For other program objectives, a goal of 80% of students passing might have been set; and for some objectives, mastery might be expected from only 20% of the students. This low expectation might correspond to the enrich-

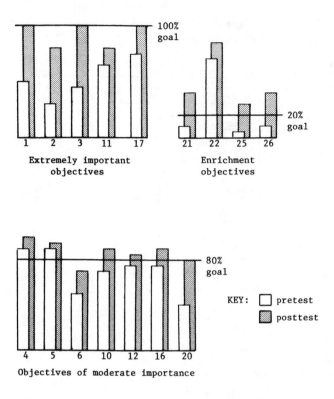

Figure 12. Achievement of program objectives showing different goals for the percentage of students achieving the objectives

ment part of a curriculum. Pass rate expectations provide a way of *grouping* objectives as is illustrated in the example. Figure 12 also shows a particularly clear way of displaying pre- and posttest pass rates; posttest results are graphed as a shadow bar *behind* the pretest bar for each objective.

You can readily see from the figure that

- the goal of 100% passing was not reached for objectives 2 and 11,
- the goal of 80% passing was not achieved for objective 6, and
- three goals had been achieved at pretest time—those for objectives 4, 5, and 22.

Putting a bar graph sideways is often convenient because it allows you to type labels inside the bars:

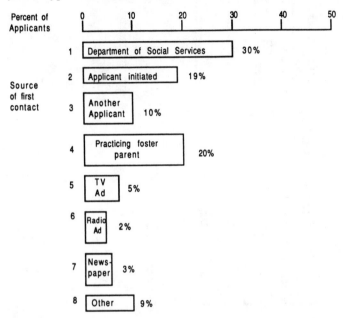

Figure 13. Percentage of Foster Parenting Program participants who first found out about the program from 8 possible sources (N = 75 applicants)

Sometimes you might not want to leave spaces between any of the bars:

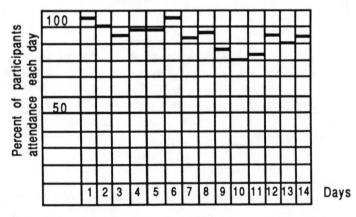

Figure 14. Participant attendance during the 14 days of the project

Sometimes you might leave out the vertical lines dividing the bars altogether:

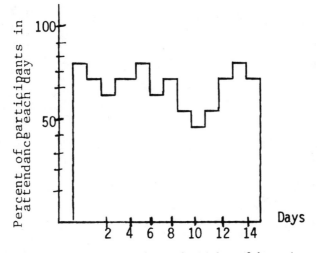

Figure 15. Participant attendance during the 14 days of the project

If the horizontal axis represents a measure that has a natural sequence, such as time or scores, you may wish to use a *line graph* rather than bother with a bar graph:

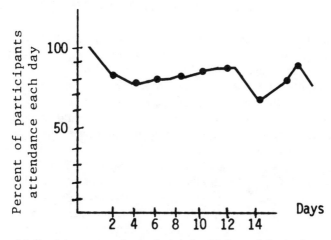

Figure 16. Participant attendance during the 14 days of the project

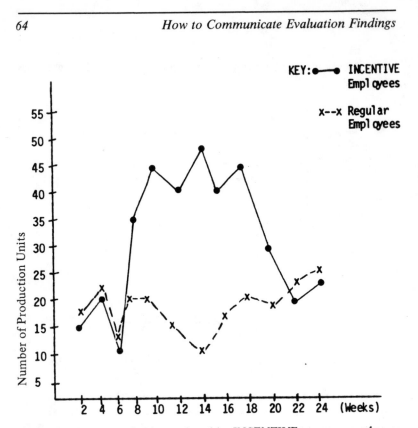

Figure 17. Number of units produced by INCENTIVE program employees and regular employees before, during, and after the INCENTIVE program

The line graph is particularly useful for showing results from *two or more* groups across time. Suppose, for example, you have production data from the experimental group, and you also want to show the production data of a comparison group. The two lines can easily be displayed together in the same graph, as in Figure 17. Superimposing two bar graphs would be confusing. Since the horizontal axis is divided according to weeks, you have a display of trends over time.

A *divided bar graph* is an unusual but useful way to show several categories of results at once. In such a case, the bar is drawn to a length representing 100% and then subdivided to show percentage of results in each category (see Figure 18). If the evaluator had graphed only the percentage of employees rating office communication as *poor,* little evidence of change would have been apparent. By using the divided graph to display all three responses, however, it becomes clear that the

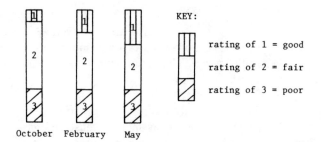

Figure 18. Percentage of employees rating office communication good, fair, or poor on 3 occasions

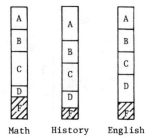

Figure 19. Distribution of teacher-assigned grades in math, history, and English for the 10th grade

proportion of *good* ratings steadily increased. It looks as if some of the employees originally responding *fair* were won over, and began to respond *good,* while the solid group of *poor* responders did not change its mind.

A divided bar graph (Figure 19) is a good way to display grade distributions. Because a grade of F is an *alarm signal,* it has been emphasized in the graph.

Showing the spread of scores

A deficiency of many graphs that show mean or average scores is that they fail to show the *dispersion* of scores—how much the scores tend to vary from the group average. This is unfortunate because indicators of score spread are easy to display.

A display of dispersion tells the audience how well the average represents the whole collection of scores. If dispersion is wide and scores vary considerably, then a mean or median must be considered less representative than when scores cluster near to it. The statistic which measures whether or not scores spread out widely around the *mean* is the standard deviation. On a *bar graph,* the standard deviation can be shown by a dotted line extending above and below the mean.

If the mean number of absences in a group was 20, with a standard deviation of 5, this could be shown in the following way:

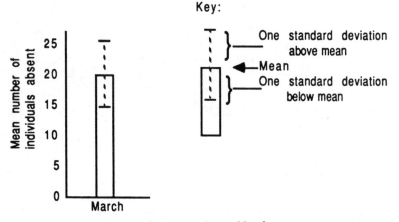

Figure 20. Mean number of absences during March

Another way to show means and standard deviations is by a *position spread graph.* It shows the position of the mean and the spread of scores around the mean via the standard deviation. The data shown in Table 16 are displayed on the position spread graph in Figure 21.

Displaying results from questionnaires

Questionnaire results can be tabulated—and therefore displayed and reported—in one of two ways.

TABLE 16
**Mean Scores on Attitude Toward Tutoring Instrument
of Students Receiving 20-Minute, 30-Minute, and 40-Minute Lessons**

| | Length of Lesson | | |
	20 mins.	30 mins.	40 mins.
Mean	14.9[a]	16.1	13.7
Standard deviation	3.5	1.8	3.4
Number of students	30	18	10

[a] Maximum score=20

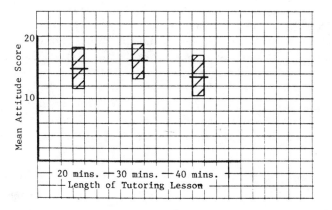

Figure 21. Mean scores on Attitude Toward Tutoring instrument of students receiving 20-minute, 30-minute, and 40-minute lessons

(1) Responses to each question are examined separately. The answers that each group of respondents made to each question are considered important enough to be displayed and discussed individually. This is the case with questions that ask about opinions or practices that are themselves either implementation or outcome objectives of the program. For example:

How often did your child bring
home work to do?   often   sometimes   never

How do you feel about the new program?

_____It's fine the way it is.   _____It's not worth saving.
_____It needs some modification.   _____Other (explain)
_____It needs extensive modifica-   _____
      tion.   _____
                                           _____

(2) Responses to two or more questions are added together or combined in some other way to produce an index of the degree to which people hold an attitude or possess a trait. This is the case with *attitude rating scales,* special questionnaires constructed by means of an item selection method that allows results from several items to be combined to yield an indicator of, say, "attitude toward school," "self-concept," or "vocational interest." The result produced by an index or attitude rating scale is a single number. Data from these instruments can be displayed using the tables and graphs described in the previous chapter.

When responses to *single questions* are to be discussed, it is customary to report *average responses* to the question per group, or *number* or *percentage* of respondents in each group answering a certain way. Averages are appropriate only for certain sorts of questions; percentages are almost universally applicable. You can report averages only where it makes sense to average—in cases where possible responses to the question reflect a *progression* in degree of attitude or behavior. For example:

How satisfied were you with the way in which information was presented?

completely   completely
dissatisfied   satisfied

  1   2   3   4   5   6   7

Reporting that people in the program group gave a mean response of 6.2 to this question (standard deviation, 0.16) allows your audience to conclude that the respondents' general attitude was favorable. Average response could not be computed for a multiple-choice question or one that asked for an answer of yes or no.

Most questions can be summarized by reporting the number or percentage per group responding a certain way. Percentages are preferred because they make it easy to compare numbers from different-sized groups.

The simplest way to present questionnaire data is to put summary statistics—the average response, or the number and percentage of persons choosing a particular response—directly onto a reproduction of the questionnaire, as shown here:

(6) How satisfied are you with the current client screening procedures?

very satisfied	fairly satisfied	dissatisfied
225 (34%)	135 (20%)	300 (45%)

Notice that in this example reporting an *average* response would have obscured the fact that respondents fell roughly into two disagreeing groups. Some were satisfied and others dissatisfied.

Questionnaires made up of *several items reported individually*, but each represented by an average, lend themselves to *line graphs,* such as Figure 22. In constructing this graph, a mean response to each question has been computed for each group. These averages were then located on a copy of the questionnaire and included in the evaluation report. The graph seems to show little difference between the responses of the E- and C-groups except that the C-group tends not to like math lab and the E-group does. These conclusions have been drawn, of course, by simply looking at the graph—"eyeballing" the data. To be strict, the significance of the difference between the mean responses to each question should be tested before firm conclusions are drawn.

If you want to display the *number or percentage of the time* certain statements were made in response to *open-ended questions,* this can be done in table form. Instruments of this type are usually scored by underlining key statements in the answer given by each respondent. After a count has been made of recurrent statements, they are paraphrased as accurately as possible, and simply listed with their frequencies.

For instance, suppose you asked this question:

(10) If there is something on your mind not covered by the questionnaire—either something you are especially pleased with or something you are concerned about—please let us know by writing in this space and on the back of the page.

Your evaluation report concerning this item would include this section:

In response to item 10, the following criticisms were expressed:

Criticism	Number of people expressing criticism
Parents were not advised of the objectives of the program	5

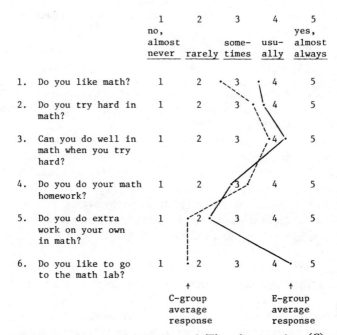

	1 no, almost never	2 rarely	3 some- times	4 usu- ally	5 yes, almost always
1. Do you like math?	1	2	3	4	5
2. Do you try hard in math?	1	2	3	4	5
3. Can you do well in math when you try hard?	1	2	3	4	5
4. Do you do your math homework?	1	2	3	4	5
5. Do you do extra work on your own in math?	1	2	3	4	5
6. Do you like to go to the math lab?	1	2	3	4	5

    ↑   ↑
C-group   E-group
average   average
response   response

Figure 22. Mean responses of experimental (E) and comparison (C) group to end-of-program math attitude questionnaire

    Parents felt they were asked to
attend meetings only to satisfy
funding requirements and not to
take part in the program planning   4

Preparing an audience to read graphs

If you must present data orally to an audience who probably knows little about graphs, gradually introduce an important graph. The presentation described in the following example will help the audience understand the information. If you suspect that the audience is fairly experienced with graphs, however, such an elementary introduction might bore them or, even worse, insult them. So be sensitive to their level of understanding and explain accordingly.

Example. An evaluator wishes to display the line graph of INCENTIVE program production rates that was shown in Figure 17 of this chapter. She wants to be sure the graph is fully understood. At first glance, projected on a screen, the graph will look confusing, so she designs a presentation that will build up to the graph. First, she shows the axes of the graph and discusses them, pointing as she talks: "This axis [the horizontal] represents work-weeks; this is the second week of January [pointing to the 2 on the axis], and these are the 10th, 16th, and the 24th weeks. For each week, the number of units produced by the employees in the INCENTIVE program were counted. The same was done for employees not in the program.

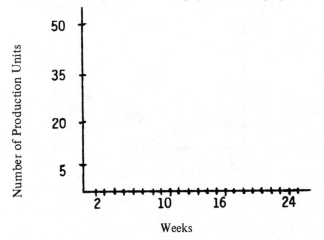

Picture 1

"Production units are shown by the vertical axis. Suppose there was one group of employees, say Group A, who produced much more than another group, Group B. Then on the graph, their production rates might look like this:

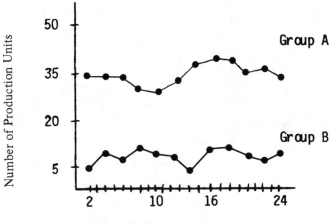

Picture 2

"Suppose that production increased steadily throughout the year. Then we'd see a rising line during the six weeks, like this:

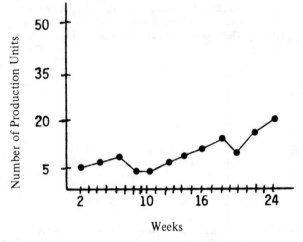

Weeks

Picture 3

"The line is drawn zigzag because there are always ups and downs, but the general trend is up, as you can see.

"Now suppose the company at week 10 did something to increase the production rate. Perhaps they hired twice as many employees. Then we'd expect the line to rise somewhere right at or after week 10.

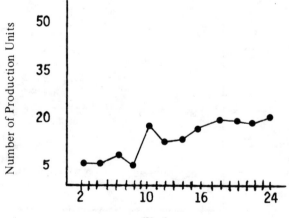

Weeks

Picture 4

"If, at the beginning of the INCENTIVE program we're talking about today, we saw a rise like that, we'd recognize that a higher production rate coincided with the beginning of the project and think that perhaps the project may have had something to do with the improvement.

"Now here are the actual graphs of the number of units produced by INCENTIVE employees and those not in the program:

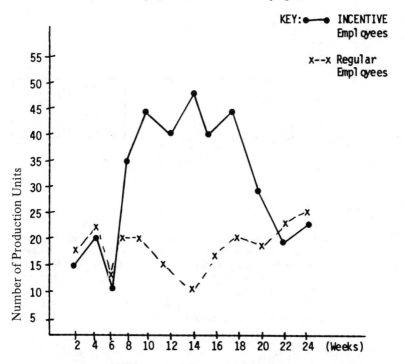

Figure 23. Number of units produced by INCENTIVE program employees and regular employees before, during, and after the INCENTIVE program

"Notice how the production rate for INCENTIVE employees increased noticeably during the project right from its beginning. Then after the project, it gradually dropped to being as high as the regular employees' levels, slightly lower than those who were not in the INCENTIVE program."

Here is another example, a brief one, in which the evaluator takes time to introduce the units used for graph-percentile ranks, because his particular approach to interpreting percentiles may not be familiar to his audience.

Example. An evaluator wishes to show a parent advisory group the progress made by the district in improving students' percentile scores on a state-mandated achievement test. He has chosen the following novel way to represent percentile data:

"On a test whose scores have been converted to percentiles, a person can score anywhere from 0 to 100. Tests scored this way are set up so that a huge

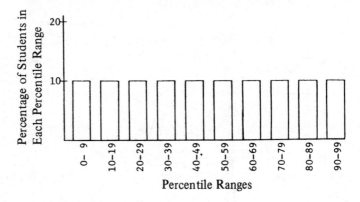

Picture 5

national testing would put 10% of all students into each of the 10 score categories shown here, 0 to 9, 10 to 19, and so on. A graph of a nationwide testing, or from a school district with an average or normal range of students, would look like this:

"That is, 10% of the students would be found in the top percentile range, 90-99 percentile, and 10% in each of the other divisions.

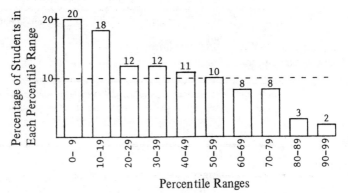

Picture 6

"However, our school district performed below average last year, and the distribution we produced is shown here:

"We have *more students* in the lower achievement categories, the lower percentiles, than an average district would have, and we have correspondingly fewer students in the high categories. The aim of our program this year, then, has been to try to make our distribution look more like the first diagram and less like the second.

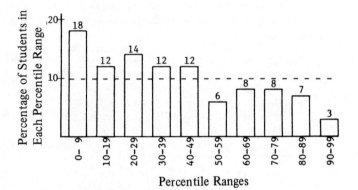

Picture 7

"Here are the results for this year. You can see we are getting closer to that 10% line right across the board":

Presenting Data: A Summary

A glance through this chapter should give you some ideas about building tables and drawing graphs for an evaluation report. In particular, you are offered this advice:

(1) Use graphic methods of presenting numerical data whenever possible.
(2) Build the results and discussion section of the evaluation report—and perhaps other sections as well—around tables and figures. Prepare the tables and graphs first; then write text to explain them.
(3) Make each table and figure self-explanatory. Use a clear, complete title, a key, labels, footnotes, and so forth.
(4) Discuss in the text the major information to be found in each table and figure.
(5) Play with, and consider using, as many graphs as you have the time and ingenuity to prepare. Not only do they communicate clearly to your audiences; they also help *you* to see what is happening.

(6) Since graphs tend to convey fewer details than numerical tables, you may sometimes wish to provide tables *and* graphs for the same data.

(7) If you have used a mixed evaluation design with both quantitative and qualitative data collection procedures, use the direct quotations and descriptions from the qualitative results to add depth and clarity to information reported graphically.

(8) When presenting complicated graphs to a live audience, give some instruction about how to read the graph and a few sample interpretations of simpler versions. Then present the real data.

(9) When a complete draft of the report has been completed, ask yourself the following questions:

- Is the title a comprehensive description of the figure? Could someone leafing through the report understand the graph?
- Are both axes of every graph clearly labeled with a name?
- Is the interval size marked on all axes of graphs?
- Is the number of cases on which each summary statistic has been based indicated in each table or on each graph?
- Are the tables and figures labeled and numbered throughout the report?
- If the report is a lengthy one, have you provided a List of Tables and Figures at the front of the report following the Table of Contents?

Note

1. Results from objectives-based tests are usually displayed via a bar graph, such as those on pages 58 to 61. Results from a true control group evaluation design, though they can be analyzed and presented in various supplementary ways, are first presented using the format of Table 7, page 54. Information about graphs and tables for presenting data from various designs and types of tests and attitude instruments can be found in *How to Design a Program Evaluation* and *How to Measure Attitudes*, Volumes 3 and 6 of the *Program Evaluation Kit*.

Reference

Anderson, S. B., & Ball, S. (1980). *The profession and practice of program evaluation.* San Francisco: Jossey-Bass.

Chapter 4
An Evaluation Report Outline

This chapter presents an outline of a formal evaluation report. The outline may be used in several ways. If you are required to write a technical report, then you might follow the outline quite closely. Simply name each section of your report according to the headings listed, and answer the questions under each heading in as much detail as you feel necessary. This exercise will give you a working draft of the report.

On the other hand, if the form of your report is not prescribed, or if your reporting can be less formal, then you will use this chapter differently—as a checklist of contents for an evaluation report or of points you may want to include. You can then organize what you say according to your own needs, with the assurance that you are not omitting important information.

Whatever the case, consider the outline as suggestive; and drop questions, perhaps amplify some of them, or add your own questions as you see fit.

Front Cover

The front cover should provide the following information:

- title of the program and its location
- name of the evaluator(s)
- period covered by the report
- date the report is submitted

Make the front cover attractive, formatted precisely. The cover reflects you and the quality of your work.

Section I. Summary

Sometimes called the *executive summary*, this important section of the report is a brief overview of the evaluation, explaining why it was conducted and listing its major conclusions and recommendations. The summary is designed for people who are too busy to read the full report; therefore, it should not be longer than two or three pages. Although the summary is placed first, it is the section that you *write* last.

Typical content

- What was evaluated?
- Why was the evaluation conducted?
- What are the major findings and recommendations or options which you conclude from the evaluation?

If space permits, add the following information:

- Were there decisions to be made on the basis of the evaluation? If so, what decisions?
- To what audiences is the evaluation report addressed?
- Who else might find it interesting or important?
- What were the major constraints, if any, under which the evaluation was conducted?

Section II. Background Information
Concerning the Program

This section sets the program in context. It describes how the program was initiated and what it was supposed to do. The amount of detail presented here will depend on the audience and the people for whom the evaluation report is prepared. If the audience has no knowledge of the program, it must be fully described. If, on the other hand, the evaluation report is mainly intended for internal use and its readers are likely to be familiar with the program, this section can be fairly brief, setting down information "for the record."

Regardless of the audience, if the report will be the sole lasting record of the program, then this section should contain considerable detail about the goals and objectives and its critical components. A preliminary description of the program should be drafted *at the time the evaluation is planned.* This will mean less work later, particularly at the busy time when the data have been collected and must be analyzed. It will also ensure for the evaluator, from the beginning, a clear grasp of the program—its critical components and what they are supposed to accomplish. If you are a summative evaluator, consider drafting Section II as soon as possible after accepting the role of evaluator, or you may have to include such a description in your evaluation proposal.

Information helpful in writing this section can be gathered from myriad sources: a program plan or proposal, needs assessment reports, discussions with program personnel, minutes of staff or board of directors meetings, memos, curriculum outlines, lists of goals, budget estimates, and so forth. The program director and staff probably have most of the information for this section in their heads, but reference to documents such as those listed will help you assess the consistency of their recollections with official program descriptions. It is important that you locate any *discrepancies* between recollections and program descriptions and resolve them before you write your report.

Typical Content

A. Origin of the program

- Where was the program implemented? What sort of communities or special groups? How many people did it affect?
- In what *aggregate* did people participate? For example, was it more appropriate to consider participants in terms of districts, schools, classrooms, or individuals?
- How did the program get started?
- Was a formal or informal *needs assessment* conducted, and if so, what were the results?
- What was the primary impetus for the program? Community, state, or national demands? Legal requirements? Opportunities for funding? Staff initiative?

B. Goals of the program

- What was the program designed to accomplish?
- What goals or objectives were set? What was their order of priority, if any?
- Especially in the case of a qualitative evaluation, were there important *unstated* or implicit goals or unanticipated effects which the evaluator identified?

C. Clients involved in the program

- What are the characteristics of the intended clients of the program (for example, age, socioeconomic status, experience, special needs, ability level)?
- On what bases were participants selected for the program?
- What was the program supposed to look like? A table such as the one on page 49 might describe this.
- Were participants to remain in the program for its duration? If not, what criteria would determine the time of their entrance or exit?

D. Characteristics of the program materials, activities, and administrative arrangements

- What *materials* were to be used, and how? Were they to be purchased or produced by the program staff?
- What *resources*—funds, physical facilities, transportation—were to be available, and who was to provide them?
- In what *activities* were program participants expected to take part?
- What specific *procedures,* if any, were program implementers to follow?
- What was the *rationale* underlying the program? That is, why did the program's planners feel that the program materials and activities would lead to the achievement of program goals?
- How highly prescribed was program implementation? How much was the program expected to *vary* from site to site or from time to time?
- How was the program managed or administered? What offices or roles were created or expanded? Who filled them? Did this represent a departure from usual practice?
- To what extent does this section describe the program as it was *supposed* to look as opposed to how it did look? Section IV, the "Results" portion of the report, may contain further information supporting the accuracy of the program description reported here.

E. Staff and others involved in the program

- How many specific personnel such as administrators, consultants, secretaries, clerks, specialists, volunteers, or others were active in the program? What roles did they assume?
- Were they required to have special training or credentials either before or during the program?
- How much time (per week, day, month, or year) did they devote to the program?

Section III. Description of the Evaluation Study

The first part of this section describes and delimits the assignment that the evaluator has accepted. It explains *why* the evaluation was conducted, what it was intended to accomplish, and what it was *not* intended to accomplish. Prepare the description of the purposes of the evaluation immediately after accepting the job as evaluator. A draft of this statement should be agreed upon by all interested parties and should be kept on file.

The remainder of this section describes the methodology of the evaluation—*how* the program was evaluated. It is important that this description be detailed; if people are to have faith in the conclusions of the evaluation, they need to know how the information was obtained. However, keep the discussion of technical matters comprehensible to an average reader. Samples of all instruments should be made available, with the exception of widely used published tests or tests which by law may not be reproduced. Samples can be placed in an appendix, but it is helpful to the reader to have a few typical items reproduced in the body of the text.

Section III should be drafted when the evaluation is being planned, and it is a good idea to circulate a copy of Sections II and III to program personnel. After all, they are expected to cooperate with the evaluation and in some cases to act on its results. They should understand how the evaluation is being conducted. If they are going to object to any practices, then you should find this out early when necessary changes can be made, rather than later when the evaluation cannot be altered. You should elicit from the program staff agreement that your evaluation will provide a fair measure of their program.

Typical Content

Four major topics should be addressed: purposes of the evaluation, evaluation designs, outcome measures, and implementation measures.

A. Purposes of the evaluation

- Who requested the evaluation?
- Was the evaluation required to be primarily formative or summative?
- If the evaluation was undertaken to enlighten a particular audience or audiences, who were they? The program staff? Legislators? Community groups? A board of directors? A regulatory agency? Parents?
- What kind of information did the audience require?
- Was the evaluation undertaken to provide information needed for a decision? If so, who were the decision makers, and what was the nature of the decisions to be made? A decision might be a choice between alternate programs; or it might be a decision to continue, discontinue, or modify all or part of the program.
- Did the evaluation aim to answer research questions? If so, state them in this section.
- What was the context in which the evaluation was conducted? Were there restrictions, constraints on time or money, or other limitations placed on the study? Were there particular issues that the evaluator agreed *not* to address?

B. Evaluation designs[1]

- Did one basic evaluation design underlie all assessments made? Were additional designs used? A combination of quantitative and qualitative approaches?
- Why were these particular designs chosen?
- What were the limitations of the designs used?
- What unavoidable confounds or contaminations were foreseen? What precautions were taken to avoid them? To what effect?
- Did certain circumstances prevent the use of more rigorous designs?
- What are your strongest justifications for the design and methods you have selected?

C. Outcome measures

Instruments or approaches used

- What program results, outcomes, or activities were measured, described, or observed? Were these results or activities mentioned among the program's goals, or did you choose to measure them for some other reason?
- For each outcome of interest, what data were collected? What instruments were used?
- Were the instruments developed by program personnel or were they purchased? If developed, how? If selected for purchase, on what basis?
- How were instruments assessed for reliability, validity, examinee appropriateness, and relevance to the program?

Data collection procedures

- What was the schedule for data collection? When were instruments administered or observations or interviews conducted and who collected the data? This can be presented in a table, such as Table 3. If necessary, justify the qualifications of those people who collected the data.
- Was training provided for those making various measurements or observations? If so, how much and what kind of training?
- Was every participant in every group measured or observed, or were sampling procedures used? What was the rationale behind the sampling procedures?

D. Implementation measures

Instruments and data collection approaches used

- Why was implementation described? To hold the program *accountable* or compliance to a proposal, plan, or philosophy of operation? Or simply to *describe* what happened?

- What crucial aspects of the program were observed, recorded, or otherwise measured? Why did you choose to focus on these features of implementation and not others?
- How were backup data collected to support your description of what the program looked like in operation? Through reading program documents, observing formal interviews or conversing with the staff? Or were other data collection methods used?
- How were instruments, if any, developed? Were commercial forms borrowed or purchased? From whom, and on what basis?
- What limitations or deficiencies were there in the instruments or in other data collection approaches?
- Were checks made on their reliability, validity, and appropriateness to the setting?

Data collection procedures

- What was the schedule for the collection of implementation information, and who collected it? A table often serves to represent a schedule.
- What training was provided, and what precautions were taken in the use of the instruments or on other data collection procedures?
- Was a representative *sampling* of the program chosen for observation? Were instruments (questionnaires, interviews) administered to everyone or only to some representative staff members?
- What limitations or deficiencies were there in the procedures used for measuring or observing implementation?

Section IV. Results

This section presents the results of the various measurements, observations and other data collection methods, described in Section III, which were used to assess outcomes and program implementation. This section might also include anecdotal evidence, testimonials about the program, or excerpts from interview transcripts. This kind of evidence enlivens the report and often conveys the quality of the program and its results in a way that cannot be expressed as numbers. While a glowing letter from one participant does not show that the program was a success for everyone, it may communicate vividly some of the program's typical strengths.

Before you begin to write the results section, all data should have been analyzed, recorded in tables, graphed or plotted, and tested for significance where appropriate. Scores from tests are usually presented in graphs and tables showing means and standard deviations for each group. Results of questionnaires are frequently summarized on a copy of the questionnaire itself.

The nature of the evaluation questions you were to answer may have required qualitative methods of data collection such as in-depth, open-ended interviews, direct observations, or case studies. The rich, detailed information should be organized or focused according to major themes, categories, or case examples. Identify direct quotations or pure descriptions of people, activities, and interactions which best portray a picture of the program as it is perceived *by those involved in it*. Organize case data into case records from which case studies and analyses can be drawn. *How to Use Qualitative Methods in Evaluation* by Michael Q. Patton (Volume 4 of the *Program Evaluation Kit*) explains how to organize case studies. The most important thing to remember is to *focus* the data. If you try to report it all, you will drown the reader in detail.

If raw data were processed and analyzed in a large number of ways or using special procedures which require explaining, then a section headed "Data Analysis Procedures" should be added between Sections III and IV. However, for most evaluations, data analysis can be presented in Section IV as the results from each instrument are reported.

Typical Content

Two types of results should be addressed in this section: results of implementation study and results of outcome study.

A. Results of implementation study

- Did the staff deliver the program which was proposed?
- Was the program implemented as planned and as the users expected? If not, what happened? Were some components dropped or modified? Were all materials available, and were they used? Was the program given to the participants for whom it was intended? Did crucial activities in fact occur?
- In as much detail as possible, describe what the program finally looked like. A table might describe this adequately, or entire activities might be described in detail because they represent typical program experiences. In qualitative evaluations, these descriptions are written narratives which provide a holistic view of the program.
- If alterations occurred in the program, what effects did they have on staff and participants' attitudes, the efficiency of operation, or other aspects of the program?
- How similar was the program from site to site? What variations occurred?

B. Results of outcome study

- How many and which participants took pretests, if they were given?
- How many of those who took pretests were still in the program group (or control group, if there was one) at the end of the program? Was there a

difference in the percentage of participants leaving the program and control groups over the program's duration? Use an attrition table, page 53, to summarize this.

- What were the results of pretests? Was there a difference in pretest scores among program and comparison groups?
- For *each measurement or observation made,* what were the final results for program participants and for participants in the comparison groups? How do they compare? Are differences statistically significant for quantitative measures? Are they practically significant? A table or graph may best summarize quantitative results.
- If there was no control group, how much did program group performance change from test to test?
- If there was no control group, to what can results be compared in order to judge their quality? For example, test norms, past performance, or standards set to reflect different levels of competence may be used for such purposes of comparison. Can comparisons be shown graphically?
- What were the results of statistical tests designed to answer questions about correlations among participants or program characteristics? See page 53 for a discussion of graphs and tables for expressing correlations.

Section V. Discussion of Results

Interpretation of each result could occur in Section IV, where the results are presented. However, if the program and/or the evaluation is complicated, a separate section for interpreting and discussing the results makes the report more clear. The results should be discussed with particular reference to the purposes of the evaluation listed in Section III.A.

Typical Content

There are two major issues to be addressed in this section: How certain is it that the program caused the results? How good were the results of the program?

A. How certain is it that the program caused the results?

- Are there alternative explanations of program results? For example, were the gains made by program participants perhaps simply the result of maturation? Were there confounds that need to be considered? If there was a control group, was there any contamination? Attempt here to anticipate and answer arguments against your attribution of program results that might be raised by a skeptic.

B. How good were the results of the program?

- How did the program results compare with what might have been expected had there been no program?
- If a control group was used, were the program results better than control group results? If the difference was statistically significant, was the size or quality of the difference enough to make it practically significant? If the difference was not statistically significant, did program results at least appear promising? Qualitative analysis does not have the handy statistical significance tests to tell the user how seriously to take the findings. The qualitative evaluator must make substantive judgments about the strengths and weaknesses of various parts of the analysis. Which patterns in the data might be "strongly supported by the evidence" and which patterns not so clearly substantiated?
- If there was no control group, how do results compare with whatever standard for judging their quality has been established?
- Does the staff feel the program would achieve more significant gains were it to be modified or run for a longer period of time? Is there evidence in your data to support this point of view?
- What were perceived as the strengths and weaknesses of the program? What conclusions or recommendations can be made from correlational studies or other observations? Do certain program features, for example, seem most effective with certain groups? Are attitudes or achievement related to participants' characteristics?

Section VI. Costs and Benefits

This optional section takes a close look at the program budget, an area fraught with controversy. There is as yet no consistently agreed upon way to collect, analyze, or present cost-benefit information, so in this section you will do the following:

(1) Justify the usefulness of the particular approach to cost benefit analysis you have taken, and
(2) present and interpret your data.

If costs and benefits are a major focus of your evaluation, you might want to include cost and benefit data in the "Results" section, with discussion integrated into Section V.

A cost-benefit discussion essentially lists the dollar costs associated with the program and then broadens into a summary of other non-dollar, qualitative costs. The benefits of the program are then described and weighed against these costs. If possible, provide in this section a *table* listing costs and benefits.

Typical Content

A. The method used to calculate costs and benefits

- How have you defined *costs* and *benefits?*
- What method have you used to compute costs and benefits? Is it a formal mathematical one? Or does it rely on informal methods of contrasting costs and benefits? What precedents can you cite for using this method?

B. Costs associated with the program

Dollar costs

- What extra monies were required to implement the program? What was the source of these funds?
- What would the money have been used for had it not been used in the program?
- What portion of the money spent on the program represents operating costs; what were the program's *start-up* costs? (The latter will not be needed if the program is continued.) A table showing program dollar expenses should be included.

Non-dollar costs

- Did the program take a toll on teacher, parent, student, or administrator patience, morale, and the like?
- Did participants work overtime because of the program?
- Were there volunteers whose time was used by the program? If so, what would they have been doing had they not been working in the program?
- Did participation in the program deprive participants of other valuable experiences?
- What other costs did the program produce either through bad morale or by using up resources or causing the loss of alternative opportunities?

C. Benefits associated with the program

Dollar benefits

- What income was received in support of or as a result of the program? For example, did the state reimburse the district for a special education program?

Non-dollar benefits

- For what positive results do you have evidence?
- How much progress was made toward program goals?
- Were outcomes for people in the program significantly better than for similar individuals not in the program?

- How big a difference did the program make?
- How much was the program valued by various groups?
- Were there any unanticipated benefits due to the program at the program site or in the broader community?

Section VII. Conclusions, Recommendations, and Options

It may be more compelling to present this section in the form of a list rather than as a narrative. The recommendations or options can be the most influential part of the evaluation report. Be sure, therefore, to emphasize what is important, and to make clear which conclusions have been *tentatively* rather than *firmly* drawn. Take care that this section attends to all the concerns that were described in detail in Section III.A, your description of the purposes of the evaluation.

Typical Content

A. Conclusions

- What are the major conclusions to be drawn about the effectiveness of the program as a whole? Of its various subcomponents? How firm are these conclusions?
- Must judgment be withheld regarding some aspects of the program?
- Did the evaluation overlook features or effects of the program that should have been considered in order to provide a complete picture of its impact?

B. Recommendations or options regarding the program

Unfortunately, many times the only part of an evaluation report that is read is the section dealing with recommendations and options. For this reason, you should prepare the section very carefully. Recommendations generally suggest a single course of action armed at remedying weaknesses in the program and perpetuating strengths. You may prefer, instead, to provide the users with *options* for alternative courses of action. Each option is supported by major findings and data from the evaluation. Based on criteria of relevance to the key evaluation questions—validity, reliability, and objectivity—the evaluator judges whether or not the data or findings are significant or important. From these judgments, the evaluator develops specific recommendations or options for actions. Recommendations and options should be directly related to the original purposes of the evaluation and to the aspects of the program which interest the evaluation users, particularly the program decision makers. Recommendations are not a wish list. They should follow logically from judgments made about the evaluation data. Your suggestions should be directed toward specific aspects of the program or to specific actions, and yet stated generally enough to allow the program planners or decision makers enough leeway to adjust the program in a manner appropriate to the realities of their particular clients, personnel, and program setting.

- On the basis of specific data, what recommendations or options can you suggest concerning the program? What are the program's greatest strengths and successes, and what aspects might be improved?
- Does the purpose for the evaluation lend itself to making recommendations or suggesting options? Do users simply want to identify the effectiveness of the program, or do they want to know what to do about its weaknesses as well?
- What predictions, hypotheses, or hunches are suggested by the data? What recommendations about further programs or research studies can be made?

C. Recommendations concerning subsequent evaluations

- What instruments served their purpose well and would therefore be recommended for use in subsequent evaluations of this or similar programs?
- Should some instruments or evaluation procedures be modified or discarded for subsequent evaluations?
- Should some components of the overall program be separately evaluated?
- If this evaluation has not been able to provide firm answers to some questions raised about the program, what evaluation procedures could yield such answers?

Note

1. An evaluation *design* is a plan determining *when* evaluation instruments (tests, questionnaires, observations, record inspections, interviews, etc.) will be administered and *to whom*. Design provides a basis for comparing results of measurement to a standard.

For Further Reading

American Psychological Association. (1983). *Publication manual of the American Psychological Association* (3rd ed.). Washington, DC: Author.

Anderson, S. B., & Ball, S. (1980). *The profession and practice of program evaluation*. San Francisco: Jossey-Bass.

Braskamp, L. A., & Brown, R. D. (1980). *New directions for program evaluation: Utilization of evaluation information*. San Francisco: Jossey-Bass.

Campbell, M. G., & Ballou, S. V. (1978). Form and style: Theses, reports, term papers (5th ed.). Boston: Houghton Mifflin.

Dinkmeyer, D. C., & Carlson, J. (1975). *Consultation: A book of readings*. New York: John Wiley.

Ewing, D. W. (1974). *Writing for results in business, government, and the professions*. New York: John Wiley.

Fleischer, M. (1983). The evaluator as program consultant. *Evaluation and Program Planning, 6*(1), 69-76.

Glass, G. V, & Hopkins, K. D. (1984). *Statistical methods in education and psychology* (2nd ed.). Englewood Cliffs, NJ: Prentice-Hall.

Government Printing Office. (1984). *Style manual* (rev. ed.). Washington, DC: Author.

Lanham, R. A. (1979). *Revising prose*. New York: Scribner's.

Rothman, J. (1980). *Using research in organizations: A guide to successful application*. Newbury Park, CA: Sage.

Smith, N. L. (1982). *Communication strategies in evaluation*. Newbury Park, CA: Sage.

University of Chicago. (1975). *A manual of style* (12th ed.). Chicago: University of Chicago Press.

Other titles in the *Program Evaluation Kit* contain very specific information about designing program evaluations and some additional suggestions for presenting findings. *Evaluator's Handbook* (Vol. 1), *How to Design a Program Evaluation* (Vol. 3), *How to Use Qualitative Methods in Evaluation* (Vol. 4), *How to Assess Program Implementation* (Vol. 5), *How to Measure Attitudes* (Vol. 6), *How to Measure Performance and Use Tests* (Vol. 7), *How to Analyze Data* (Vol. 8).

Index

NOTES

NOTES

NOTES

NOTES